JOINT
CUSTODY
WITH A
JERK

JOINT CUSTODY WITH A JERK

Raising a Child with an Uncooperative Ex

A HANDS-ON, PRACTICAL GUIDE TO COMMUNICATING
WITH A DIFFICULT EX-SPOUSE

Julie A. Ross, M.A., and **Judy Corcoran**

St. Martin's Griffin
New York

For my dad, Wallace Lee Anderson
(September 2, 1922–September 22, 2009), who read
through all my manuscripts offering sage advice
and enthusiastic support. I wish he could have seen this one, too.
—JULIE A. ROSS

To Molly, my terrific daughter, for her unending patience,
love, and support, and to Dennis Clawson, Peter Thall,
and Susan Belair, who are always there for me. And to
my ex, who, after twenty-five years, turned out to be an okay guy.
—JUDY CORCORAN

CONTENTS

INTRODUCTION

*jerk\'jrk*n* **1** an ex-wife or ex-husband who continually annoys you with stupid, irrational, and immature behavior **2** one whose values differ so dramatically from yours that you wonder how you will ever make it through your child's lifetime

When we originally wrote this book, we never thought it would become the second best-selling book on divorce on amazon.com—mainly because there wasn't an amazon.com! In 1995 very few people had computers and still fewer used the Internet. What we did know, however, was that there was a substantial need for a book that could help ex-spouses communicate in the midst of a contentious divorce.

Divorce is hard on people, and it's especially hard on children. All of the best advice that was and is currently out there can be summarized by these words: Keep the children out of it. The problem, however, is that time and again a parent would say, "I'm trying, but my ex . . ." So this book is for those of you who are trying, but your ex isn't.

In the years since this book was published, it has helped

countless people learn to communicate with their difficult ex-spouses and we know that it will continue to do so. When we reviewed it recently, though, we realized that technological changes in the past fifteen years had created yet another area that needed to be addressed: the impact of the Internet and the effects of instant and constant communication.

Because the avenues for communication have multiplied, it has become especially important to learn communication skills that will enable you not only to speak to your ex face-to-face but also to expand your proficiency with other communication tools. New forms of communication, such as texting, can be helpful or hurtful, so when and how to use these other platforms are of paramount importance. Throughout the book, whether you're speaking to your ex, texting him or her, emailing or using another form of contact, you will discover practical, easy-to-learn techniques that will move you from insults and blame to cooperative communication.

We think you'll see more hope in this edition than in the original. After all, we've had fifteen additional years of dealing with joint custody issues and practicing the principles we suggest in the book, and we've seen the progress and results. Children do grow up, exes do remarry, and most of the time, parents do move on to a place where they can, at least, share in the pride of their child's many accomplishments and appreciate the efforts everyone has made.

We would like to thank the many people who made this book possible by supporting our ideas and sharing their stories with us. You will notice in this book that we alternate randomly between the pronouns "he" and "she" when referring to jerks, exes, husbands, wives and children. We know that there can be more than one child per family, but for simplicity's sake, we often pared the examples down to situations between a parent and one child.

We would also like to thank Emilie Ross and Dennis Clawson for helping us with the manuscript, since the original version was lost on an ancient computer. And finally, we offer a special thanks to our agent, Bob Levine, and to our editor, Jennifer Weis—a big thanks for making this happen.

Julie and Judy

1.

What Did I Ever See in My Ex?

My son thinks his dad can do no wrong. But my ex lies to us all the time. He says he can't pick up our son on Saturday morning because he has to work. When I call his office to offer to drop Danny off, he's not there. It makes me crazy!

My ex is constantly changing her plans and then expects me to change mine. I'm really tired of it. But what can I do? If my ex cancels visitation at the last minute, I can't leave the kids alone.

My ex is big on Facebook and Twitter, and he's all over it with the kids and what they do each weekend, posting photos or reporting: "Here we are at the park" or "Here we are at the zoo." I miss my kids terribly on weekends and this just makes me miss them more. How can I get him to leave the kids out of his Facebook life?

The trailers for the new blockbuster movie looked great and I really wanted to take my son. I couldn't take him to the opening, though, because his dad had him then, so we agreed that we'd go the following weekend. But when he came home from his dad's, he told me they'd already seen it. I was told: "It was *great!*" I wanted to kill my ex!!! How dare he? My son knew that I was looking forward to seeing the movie with him and then his father pulls the rug out from under our plans. He does this all the time—he constantly undermines the fun things I have planned with our son.

When the kids go to visit their father for the weekend, it's party time. He feeds them junk, lets them stay up all night to watch R-rated movies, and has no regard for their personal hygiene. Late Sunday night, he returns them sick, tired, and dirty. I have a terrible time getting them up for school on Monday.

My ex begged for more visitation time with the kids. Now that he got what he wanted, he doesn't actually take them more often—he thinks that talking to them via Skype counts as a visit! So I still have the child-care duties and he feels like he's fulfilled his paternal duties by video chatting.

When we were married, my husband and I vowed to never look at each other's email. Well, now that he's broken all those other vows, I don't think I need to honor this one completely. I changed my password the day he left, but he's never bothered to change his. And while I don't open his emails, I sometimes log onto his account to see if he's read the ones I've sent him. And I read the subject lines. So now I've figured out that he's dating someone and I think he's looking to buy a house. But when I ask him if he's dating someone and thinking of moving, he denies it!

It's bad enough that my teenage daughter is forever on her phone, texting her friends, but on the weekends she spends with me I see her become visibly upset because her mom has texted her about something. Often it's about how much she misses her, and sometimes it's about cleaning her room. I've asked my ex to leave us alone on "my" time, but she just ignores this and calls, texts, or IMs at will.

My ex never bothers to repack my daughter's clothes, schoolwork, games, and other belongings, so we always have a big scene when she returns home and realizes that she's missing things. I'm really tired of buying her new stuff because her dad can't remember to pack them.

My ex really wants our daughter to learn piano and I couldn't care less. He's always calling me to see if she's practicing and it's making me nuts!

SHARING CUSTODY WITH A JERK

Do you find that your ex has no respect for your time or schedule, for the values you've worked so hard to instill in your child, and for the lifestyle you've developed since your divorce or separation? Does your ex sometimes act or respond in immature, inconsiderate, and irresponsible ways? Is he or she, at times, a complete jerk?

If you are raising a child with an uncooperative ex, the scenarios we just listed most likely ring true in some form or another. In fact, if your ex-husband or ex-wife is a true jerk, you can probably add a few outrageous stories of your own. But whether you're dealing with an ex who intentionally tries to manipulate you and your child or one who inadvertently confuses and complicates your life, there is help. This book offers simple yet effective tools and techniques that will help you communicate with your ex. In turn, this will change how your ex reacts and responds to you, regardless of whether he or she is an occasional or a chronic jerk. Instead of fighting and arguing about raising your child, you will soon be discussing and negotiating your child's future.

Using shared custody scenarios throughout this book, we demonstrate how these communication tools and techniques will help you solve problems and bring about change in your relationship with your ex and your child. As we go along, you will be able to substitute the details of your own particular problems into the structures we have set up to decide which course of action is best for you. We revisit the problems mentioned at the beginning of this chapter as they apply in the later chapters, so stick with us.

In this book you'll learn how to listen (as opposed to just waiting for your turn to talk), negotiate (discover win-win alternatives), teach responsibility (to your ex and your child), take responsibility yourself (without taking on the problems of others), and foster cooperation among the three (or more) of you. You'll see that all of these are crucial elements that will ensure that you and your child survive and thrive in the aftermath of your divorce.

LIFE'S MOST IMPORTANT JOB

Raising a child is one of life's most important and difficult tasks, yet most people undertake this enormous job with little or no experience or instruction. In fact, most people have had more instruction in how to drive a car than in how to parent a child or conduct an intimate relationship. How many parents give birth knowing how to teach responsibility to a child or to build self-esteem and instill values in their children in a world that is constantly changing? This is a tremendous responsibility and takes hard work even in an intact family. Then try accomplishing this job—raising a child and negotiating the minute details of that child's future—with an ex-spouse whom you no longer respect and who can be uncooperative and immature and the task can feel Herculean! Not many people would volunteer for a job like this, but your child needs you to raise your hand, step forward, and say, "Yes, I can!"

Study after study on divorce says that your child will turn out okay if you don't ask him or her to choose between you and your ex and if you provide your child with a stable home life. But if you are like most parents in the throes of a divorce, stability might not be your strong suit right now. That's why it is beneficial for you to learn and use specific techniques that will enable you to handle situations with your ex in such a way that your child isn't damaged during this unstable period of your life.

THE SCOPE OF THIS BOOK

This book deals with change. In it we present clear and practical techniques that you can use to make changes in yourself. Most of the time, the changes in your behavior will change your ex's behavior as well. However, if your ex is threatening you or your children with violence, you need to seek professional help. Exes who lose self-control are not just jerks. They have serious problems that the police and other authorities need to know about. Included in this category is constant verbal battering and emotional torment, which can be as damaging and hurtful as broken bones. An ex who engages in these kinds of behaviors is *not within the scope of this book.*

Nor do we deal with deadbeat moms and dads. We define deadbeats as those parents who physically, emotionally, and/or financially abandon their children. If your ex has run off, there are legal channels to follow. Laws are getting tougher every day in every state, but it is still difficult to engage a deadbeat, and you have our sympathy.

Finally, you'll find that we present only one person's point of view in each example. We realize that there are two sides to every story (and sometimes three!), but if your ex were willing to discuss your parenting and divorce issues with a therapist or counselor these problems would be on their way to being solved.

This book is for the person who feels that his or her ex won't even acknowledge that there's a problem, for the person who feels very alone in his or her co-parenting situation. We've written it for those of you who are ready and willing to make the changes necessary within yourselves to be effective and resourceful in dealing with the problems that arise from sharing custody with a jerk.

Know, too, that your life will get better after divorce. If you have young children, the physical aspect of parenting will get easier as they get older. And your divorce most likely presents you with an opportunity to reinvent yourself once you move past this trying time.

KEEPING IT IN PERSPECTIVE

Divorces are usually ugly. The basic process of taking everything that was "ours" and dividing it into "yours" and "mine" is a negative action. On a personal level, divorces consist of one of you telling the other that you don't want to be partners anymore.

All the plans you made won't happen now. All the sacrifices you made don't count. The vows and promises are broken, and in the middle of your life you have to start over.

Divorce also represents the end of the fantasy of living happily ever after, of having a "normal" family life, of growing old with your spouse. You may now wonder who will love you when you're old or sick and if you will ever meet someone again. You may feel like used goods. And on top of all this, your ex is a jerk!

To keep your ex's behavior in perspective, it's important to realize that everyone is capable of acting like a jerk at times. Your ex, your boss, your neighbor, your parents, and yes, even *you* possess the necessary ingredients to earn that derogatory title!

In this book, we define a jerk as someone who intentionally fouls up your plans, who doesn't think things through, and who's inconsiderate, either consciously or unconsciously. Jerks lie to you, blame you for things, don't follow through and, in general irritate you. They're selfish, spineless, and sometimes just plain stupid.

There's this guy in my office who's a real jerk. He snaps at everyone and has this condescending attitude, so everyone snaps back at him and avoids him. One day, I decided I wasn't going to play his game anymore. Now, when he asks me a question, I give him a straight answer and ignore his tone of voice or snide comments. I stopped wasting my time thinking up witty put-downs. And you know what? He dropped his tough-guy attitude and now speaks to me normally. He's still a jerk with everyone else, but we definitely get along a lot better now.

Admittedly, it's easier to deal with jerks when you have no emotional attachment to them. In all likelihood a coworker doesn't know you intimately and can't use that intimacy against you. But we all deal with jerks every day in every part of our lives. How to deal with them, rather than lamenting the fact that we must deal with them, is the issue.

DRIVING BACKWARD

Many divorced parents feel bogged down with guilt, thinking, *Maybe there was something I could have done to avoid this.* Others find themselves caught up in blaming their ex for the failed relationship, thinking, *She* [or *he*] *was the one who caused this.*

Wallowing in guilt or blame keeps you stuck in the past, examining and re-examining the details of how you found yourself in this predicament, and prevents you from moving forward and getting on with your life. It's important to be able to look at the divorce in its proper perspective, acknowledging and accepting responsibility for mistakes when it's appropriate and knowing when something's not your fault. Divorce is usually a two-way street—and an unpleasant one at that.

One of the hardest parts for me was admitting that I had been such a bad judge of character in marrying my ex. How could I have fallen in love with such a jerk? He's selfish, he doesn't tell the truth, and he runs away from his problems. I didn't think he was this way when we were married, but how could he have changed so much in the short time we've been divorced? I keep going over details in my head, trying to figure out how I was so blind to his faults.

This mother could spend her life trying to figure out whether her ex was a jerk before they married or if he turned into one after they divorced, but why waste her time? She could also spend her time berating herself and putting herself down, but again, where is that going to get her? Ruminating about the past is like trying to drive backward to undo a car accident.

IF IT WALKS LIKE A JERK . . .

It took Karen three years before she was able to put into proper perspective the roles that she and her ex had played in the divorce. Much of that time she blamed herself for their divorce and subsequent bad post-marriage relationship. She felt that her aggressiveness about custody arrangements had caused her ex to behave badly. But as the months passed, he became even more distant and uncooperative. Time after time he called to cancel visitation at the last minute or didn't show up at all. He forgot their son's birthday one year and almost never sent gifts or even visited on the major holidays. Recently, Karen had this revelation: "When I tell my friends about my ex's behavior, not one of them sticks up for my ex. You know, that tells me something. If he walks like a jerk and talks like a jerk, chances are, *he's a jerk!*"

Laura, on the other hand, found herself in the opposite scenario. For years she blamed Harry, her ex, for his emotional distance, lack of cooperation, and "underfunctioning" in both the marriage and the divorce. Not long ago she fell in love and moved in with a new man and had this insight:

> I fell in love with Jared because he was the exact opposite of Harry. He actually behaved like an "adult" and didn't rely on me to do everything for him. A few months after we moved in together, though, I realized that I was struggling with him for control, and it suddenly hit me that I have a tendency to "overfunction." I like being the "manager" in a relationship. I feel embarrassed to admit it, but I guess I was part of the problem in my marriage to Harry. When I took control, he backed off, and that contributed to what I perceived as his emotional distance and lack of cooperation.

RESPECT: A CASUALTY OF DIVORCE

At some point in your divorce, you may wonder what you ever saw in your ex. The behaviors you once thought were cute and harmless have now become irritating and unacceptable. That passionate phrase "don't stop; don't stop!" has turned into "oh, please, not that again." Your "one-and-only soul mate" is now "a complete idiot." Your "ideal woman" has become a "conniving bitch." That "hunk of a guy" is now a "stupid bastard."

When a marriage dissolves, respect for your spouse usually diminishes or disappears. Your view of your ex can change dramatically, and you may no longer appreciate his or her opinion, knowledge, and judgment. You also may not trust your ex, especially if he or she has broken the bond of trust through behavior or words. Trust and respect for your ex, which once allowed you, as a couple, to arrive at harmonious agreement, are crucial in negotiating life's daily routine. Without them, even the most serene of us are driven to occasional fury.

I knew our marriage was over when we were in couples counseling and the therapist asked me to pay my husband a compliment and I couldn't think of one, other than he could lift heavy things.

While you may never get to the point where you respect or trust your ex again, acting respectfully (and keeping your eyes open) can go a long way toward creating a healthy divorce.

YOUR HISTORY PLAYS A PART

All people bring to their marriage the entire history of their relationships with their parents, siblings, and peers. Many therapists agree that the marital bed contains six people—you, your spouse, your parents, and your spouse's parents. The theory that we re-create in our marriage what felt familiar to us as children, whether it was healthy or not, is now generally accepted. It's like the old song says: "I want a girl just like the girl who married dear old Dad." Ted's story about his initial meeting with Sarah and the ensuing impact on his marriage illustrates this very point:

When I met Sarah on a blind date ten years ago, she was forty minutes late and it didn't really bother me. She was all that I was looking for in a woman—beautiful, smart, high-powered, and successful. Everything about her really turned me on. So what if she was late? She always had a good excuse like a traffic jam or a meeting at work. My mother was the same way. As a kid, I was always the last one to get picked up from baseball practice or to arrive at birthday parties. I guess I grew up thinking that women are just always late.

During our marriage, Sarah got a little better, but that was because I watched her very closely. If I saw her sitting down with a magazine at two thirty when she was supposed to pick up Jason, our six-year-old son, at three and he was a half hour away, I'd bring it to her attention. And if we were going out, I'd sometimes tell her that we had to be there at seven thirty instead of eight, so if she started to run late we would still get there on time.

Over the years, though, her lack of regard for other people's schedules really began to bother me. And now that we're divorced, I can't put up with it anymore. She says she'll drop Jason off at one, so I make plans to go to a two o'clock movie, and she shows up at two ten. By that time, we've missed the movie and it's too late to make other plans.

Doesn't she realize that her lateness doesn't affect just me anymore; it affects Jason, and sometimes my girlfriend and even our babysitter?

It may sound odd that one of the reasons Ted was attracted to Sarah when they first met was because she was late. As he said, his mother was always late and it was familiar to him. Many marriage counselors agree that when you get married you often choose someone who either has similar qualities to one of your parents or is the polar opposite.

There are hundreds of books and theories on why we're attracted to someone—similarities, opposites, looks, scents, and so on. The adage about opposites attracting is really more about being captivated by people who have traits that you admire, which are often the traits you lack. You're drawn to people who can help you move beyond your own limitations. That's how the organizer and the disorganized end up together.

It's commonly known that people fall in love with someone who they subconsciously believe will help them resolve their childhood conflicts. By trying to fix these conflicts with your spouse you're actually trying to resolve the issues you had or have with your parents. And if you came from a dysfunctional family (and many of us did), your need to heal your childhood pain can result in very dysfunctional adult relationships.

Keep in mind that if you attracted and married a partner who was unable and unwilling to meet your marital needs, you most likely have divorced a partner who is unwilling and unable to meet your divorcing needs.

WHAT'S DONE IS STILL HAPPENING

When you get angry at your ex, only about 10 percent of your anger can be attributed to the current situation. The other 90 percent comes from your past experiences with your ex, as well as those with your parents, caregivers, and other significant people in your past. The current situation has simply triggered your past anger and allowed it to resurface. It's been said that if you're hysterical, the cause is probably historical.

That bears repeating: If you're hysterical, the cause is probably historical. Also, the longer you and your ex were together, the more extensive and rich your history. Each partner often knows precisely which button to push and exactly where to strike to intentionally hurt the other. In a divorce, the need to strike back, where it hurts most, is often present.

TED'S TIME BOMB

Sarah said she'd pick up Jason at six fifteen on Sunday. That was great because I had a date and tickets for a concert that started at seven thirty and Jason wanted to get home in time to watch a show on TV. But when the clock struck seven and I saw Jason take off his coat and turn on the TV, I hit the roof.

Sarah was full of excuses when she showed up at seven fifteen. She couldn't find her cell phone, there was an accident on the highway, and so on. I had heard it all before and I called her on it, saying she was inconsiderate, lazy, stupid—you name it. Well, as my anger increased, so did hers, and before I knew it we were swearing at each other. Then I ripped up the concert tickets and threw them on the ground. She stormed off, leaving Jason so confused and frightened that he ran after her crying.

RENEGOTIATING YOUR RELATIONSHIP

At some point, you need to face the fact that your marriage is over. Unfortunately, when children are involved, that doesn't mean that your relationship with your ex is over, too. For the sake of your children, the marital relationship must now change and develop into a parenting relationship. This change, however, is extremely challenging, in part because we get stuck believing that it's the other person's responsibility to make the changes, not ours. Yet change is necessary, and when you're dealing with an uncooperative ex it's likely that if you wait for him or her to change, it will never happen. So let's look at some of the things that might get in the way of seeing the need to make changes in ourselves. Once we begin to recognize that we need to change, we can then learn the techniques or skills that will enable us to deal more effectively with the jerks in our lives.

Among the things that prevent us from seeing a need to change are highly charged emotions such as fear, anger, and jealousy.

Fear : Fear is one of the most basic emotions. Animals sense fear before and beyond most other emotions. Some people believe that fear is the opposite of love in that other emotions, such as anger and jealousy, spring from fear—fear of losing something can make us angry or jealous; fear of injury can make us cautious; fear of not getting what we need can make us aggressive; fear of abandonment can make us clingy and needy. Fear subconsciously causes us to fight for what we need—or hightail it out of there.

Change fills many people with fear and thus prevents us from moving forward because there's a hidden payoff in keeping things the same. Familiar dynamics, even if they are abusive or hurtful, are more comfortable because we know what to expect. On the other hand, change means risking the unknown. And for most of us, fear of the unknown is more powerful than the misery of the current situation. It's the "devil you know is better than the devil you don't know" philosophy. Of course, the problem is that if you want things to be different, you have to change the way you do things. If you do something the same way over and over, you'll get the same results. If you do something the same way over and over and expect different results, you'll go crazy. The key to getting different results, therefore, is to face your fears and change how you do things in the first place.

Anger : Anger makes us feel stubborn and unwilling to change. When we're angry, we dig in our heels and deliberately do the opposite of what we're being asked, even if what we're being asked is to our ultimate benefit. Instead of clearly seeing what changes we can make to get what we want, we have a tendency to seek revenge. It's easy to allow feelings of rejection, abandonment, and betrayal to turn into anger after your divorce. And it's even easier to allow that anger to cloud your judgment about the need for change.

Jealousy : Jealousy also clouds our judgment. It can cause us to blow things out of proportion, believe things that aren't true, disregard things that are obvious and, in general, overreact. While anger sometimes clouds reality, it usually directs our actions. There's nothing directive about jealousy, however. It's like blowing a gray fog over everything. At times, it's difficult to cut through jealousy and determine whether the problem you're having with your ex is a real issue or not.

Jealousy of one's ex is common. Perhaps your ex has gone on to become successful in business while you're having financial problems. Or your ex has a very attractive new partner and you're not seeing anyone. Maybe your ex is having another baby while your biological clock is ticking away. All of these things can stir up jealous feelings, but it may help to know that it's rarely as great on the other side of the fence as it seems:

> I went into a jealous depression when my ex remarried. I didn't want to let our sons attend his wedding and wouldn't buy them suits. I had fantasies about wrapping his wife's bouquet with poison ivy and hoped she'd get eaten by a shark on their honeymoon. We still had some friends in

common, but because I was such a pest about the wedding, asking the details and so on, most of them stopped talking to me. Now it's seven years later and he's divorcing this wife, too. He's got another child, a daughter who's two, and he has to pay to support her as well. I heard that he recently moved into a studio apartment. On the other hand, things have really settled down for me. I was promoted at work and just bought a new house. And our sons, who are now twelve and fourteen, are going away to camp for two months this summer. I'm really looking forward to summer, and I'd choose my life over his any day.

Facing your fear of the unknown, getting over your anger, and looking beyond your jealousy will allow you to leap ahead!

ENDING SELF-DESTRUCTIVE SELF-TALK

In most divorces, your self-esteem takes a big hit and it often takes all you can do to rebuild it. For many, that means finding a good therapist or a self-help group. For others, it may mean starting an exercise or eating plan or getting a new job or going back to school. In any case, rebuilding self-esteem almost always involves doing things differently. While putting off change until tomorrow may be a familiar route, starting now can jump-start your self-esteem and head you in the right direction. As we said before, this book asks you to make a changes that will, in turn, affect your ex's behavior. The first change we want you to be aware of is what we call self-destructive self-talk.

All people talk to themselves. When you're walking down the street, maybe you think, *Gee, did I remember to turn off the coffeepot?* or, *I have to call that new client when I get back to the office.* That's self-talk, and it goes on in our heads much of the day. Self-talk can be productive or unproductive. Productive self-talk promotes change. We say to ourselves, *I want to get that proposal out at work today,* or, *I'm not sure I told the babysitter what time I was coming back; I'll have to call her.* Productive self-talk motivates us and can even work as a check-and-balance system.

Self-destructive self-talk, on the other hand, blocks our initiative to change and undermines our belief and confidence in ourselves. The self-destructive messages we send to ourselves often have a basis in the messages we received during childhood and frequently mimic the voices of our parents. *I am a total idiot. I can't believe I forgot that,* for example, may have originated in a childhood scolding: "What are you, an idiot? You should know better than that!" The unfortunate thing about this type of self-talk is that it diminishes your self-esteem. And when self-esteem is low, you're less likely to try new things, make new friends, and, of course, make changes in your life, including changing your relationship with your ex.

Then I start thinking that maybe I'm not such a great catch, either. After all, why would any man want to get involved with a woman with a two-year-old? Especially one who's so tired all the time. And I feel like I look awful. My house is a mess, and I just want to crawl into a hole with a box of chocolates and pull the hole in with me.

If you want your life to change, it's important that you take steps to eliminate this type of self-talk from your thoughts. To do this, you must first recognize that you speak to yourself this way. Next, you must make a conscious effort to override the self-destructive message with a constructive one. Because human beings can think only one thought at a time, self-destructive self-talk can be overridden by memorizing other, more positive thoughts and repeating those thoughts over and over to replace the negative ones. Here are some typical self-destructive self-talk phrases and suggestions for more positive expressions:

Self-Destructive: I'm a terrible parent.
Constructive: I'm a loving, caring, good parent.

Self-Destructive: I'm not very good at this.
Constructive: I'm learning to do this better.

Self-Destructive: I can't cope with this.
Constructive: I can handle this.

Self-Destructive: My ex was always better at this than me.
Constructive: My way is different, and it's just as good.

Self-Destructive: I don't care how others see me. I'm a
    loser all around!
Constructive: If I put on clean clothes, I will feel better
    about myself.

If you feel the negative thought trying to creep back in, try saying to that voice, "I appreciate your comments on the situation, but I'm going to listen to this other thought right now." When you become proficient at getting rid of your negative inner voices, you will free yourself for the positive alternatives. Seeing these alternatives promotes change.

POST-CRISIS GOALS

Another component that prevents change is the amount of stress you're under at the moment. There are times of crisis in everybody's life, and if you're undergoing a divorce or other major changes in your life, consider yourself in crisis. You may feel lonely, overwhelmed, and even doomed, and like the emotions of fear, anger, and jealousy, these intense feelings can become major obstacles to change.

Crises often seem more manageable and less overwhelming if you think of them as having a beginning, a middle, and an end. By identifying where you are in the "crisis transition," you can more easily see that eventually the crisis will be over. Ask yourself, "When this is over, what do I want?"

Making a list of your post-crisis dreams can help you focus and encourage you to move forward. Maybe you'd like a bigger apartment, more money, a new job. Listing these things can help you clarify that there is life after crisis (and after divorce) and will help you determine how to move forward and change to achieve your goals.

It may also help if, alongside your list of post-crisis goals, you make a list of things that you're grateful for. This "gratitude list" sometimes helps you keep the crisis in perspective, to see that maybe, just maybe, you're not doomed after all. Maybe there is a little light in your life right now, with more to come.

WHEN "I DO" TURNS INTO "I DON'T HAVE TO ANYMORE"

We've all heard the statistics. The fact is that about 50 percent of all marriages end in divorce and, according to the U.S. Census, about 33 percent of our nation's households are headed by single parents. Experts say that 50 to 60 percent of all children will spend some time in a single-parent home.

When a marriage breaks up, the following months and even years can be turbulent for everyone involved. But the dust does eventually settle as new routines and rituals become the norm. For many, though, the problems of creating a new household, dividing the parental responsibilities, and sharing custody feel as though they'll take a lifetime to resolve. It's helpful, and hopeful, to note that no problem is too big to be solved if it is viewed in its proper perspective and broken down into addressable issues.

In the next few chapters, we discuss how to break down complex problems into manageable pieces and how to know what to do and how to do it once you've identified the changes that need to be made. In short, we give you a toolbox full of tools for dealing with your ex in typical confrontations that will invite him or her to respond to you in a more positive and productive way.

2.

Identifying the Problem
(Other Than Your Ex Is a Jerk)

IT'S ALWAYS SOMETHING

Buddha said, "Life is suffering." Similarly, Dr. M. Scott Peck begins his internationally acclaimed book, *The Road Less Traveled,* by saying: "Life is difficult" and goes on to say that once we truly understand and accept that life is problematic, it becomes easier, because the fact that it's difficult no longer matters. As for solving these problems, Dr. Peck says: "We cannot solve life's problems except by solving them." But first, we must acknowledge that there is a problem.

DEALING WITH DENIAL

Denial, which comes in many forms, is one way to deal with problems. To paraphrase Charles Schulz, the creator of the comic strip *Peanuts,* there's no problem too big to run away from!

Denial is a common element in divorced parenting. Often one parent sees a problem very clearly while the other denies that it exists at all. The problem with denial, of course, is that it effectively delays us from finding solutions to our problems. Yet many people cling to denial as if it were a cloak that makes them invisible and protects them from future consequences.

Your ex may be one of those people who practices denial. Even if you were to hire a jet to write: "There's a problem here!" across the sky, if your ex is in denial, it's clear that you'll get no help from him or her in solving that problem. After all, why should your ex want to fix something that he or she feels isn't broken in the first place? To get around this, you will have to engage in some creative problem-solving techniques in order to get the solution you want.

Before a problem can be solved, it must be correctly identified. Often, problems are so complex that their clarification requires several steps.

Step 1: *Identifying Your Feelings*

When Jenny arrived home from spending the weekend with her dad, the first thing I noticed was that her suitcase was bulging. As I opened it, I wondered what my ex had bought for her this time. Inside was a complete Swiss mountaineer outfit, made of gray suede with little pink and blue flowers embroidered on the child-sized suspenders. I'm embarrassed about this now, but I exploded in anger and went screaming to Jenny, asking her where this outfit came from. When she answered, "Daddy brought it back from his trip," that's when I really lost it. *So that's where he was last weekend—skiing in*

Switzerland! I thought to myself. *And he said he was working. What a jerk!* I flung the tiny outfit across the room and was dumping the rest of the suitcase's contents on the floor when Jenny came in, asking what was the matter with me. She looked so sweet when she asked, "Don't you like the outfit Daddy brought me?"

Jenny's mom, Samantha, knew that her reaction to finding the gift was out of line, but it wasn't until she calmed down and thought about it that she realized why she was so upset. In her eyes, the expensive outfit was a waste of money. Jenny would never wear it. But more important than that was the fact that Samantha was angry because her ex was able to take a trip to Switzerland. They had planned to go skiing there six years earlier and then she'd gotten pregnant with Jenny, so they had postponed the trip. Then came the divorce. Not only was Samantha jealous that her ex had finally gotten to go, but she also was so busy at work that she couldn't go away now or even in the near future.

SEPARATING THE FEELINGS FROM THE PROBLEMS

It's important to separate your feelings from the problems that cause you to have those feelings. For example, the problem here isn't that Samantha's ex is a jerk—at least not in this case. In fact, he's done something rather nice in bringing back a gift for his daughter. But Samantha's anger and disappointment are causing her to label him a jerk. In this case, though, "jerk" is how she feels about him. Feelings are different from facts. Samantha's not having the time to go to Switzerland is both a fact and a problem. Jealousy that her ex got to go on "their" trip is a feeling.

Feelings become problems only if you act on them inappropriately. Feeling vengeful toward your ex is not a problem. Enacting revenge by pelting his car with rotten eggs is a problem because you acted on your negative feelings.

Many times problems are not only complex but also charged with intense feelings such as anger and jealousy. When feelings overwhelm us, one of two things often happen: We either react in an explosive way like Samantha did by yelling, flinging the outfit across the room, and dumping the contents of the suitcase on the floor or we become paralyzed by our emotions. Either situation makes us less effective in clearly viewing the various components of a complex issue.

Step 2: Naming and Claiming Your Feelings

In situations where you experience very intense feelings, it helps to ask yourself what's behind those feelings. Can you isolate an instance in your history, in your marriage, or in your childhood where something like this happened? Are you holding a grudge? Is your ex treating you the way your parents treated you? Are you expecting something from your ex that you really don't think he or she can deliver? Are you frightened that this situation will escalate? Are you feeling helpless? Are you, as Samantha was, jealous?

All people experience a large assortment of feelings, yet most have trouble labeling their subtle emotions with the correct feeling word. It's like understanding a language when someone speaks it to you but not knowing which words to use in reply.

Most of us have a tendency to generalize our feelings into four main categories: anger, depression, fear, and happiness. We say, "I'm furious at him"; "I'm so angry at her, I could kill her"; "I'm so depressed"; "I'm too scared"; "I'm feeling happy today." Negative feelings get categorized as anger. Helpless, hopeless, or sad feelings are labeled depression. Anxieties are grouped as fear, and any positive feelings are termed happiness. These main categories end up masking the true, subtler emotions that underlie them, and there's a big difference between being "annoyed" and being "furious."

Take a look at the following list of feeling words:

accepted	boastful	concerned
adequate	bold	confident
adventurous	bored	confused
afraid	brilliant	conniving
aggressive	calm	contemptuous
amused	caring	content
angry	cautious	cranky
anxious	cheated	crazy
apathetic	cheered	creative
ashamed	comfortable	daring
bashful	competitive	defeated

defiant	greedy	loving
delighted	guilty	martyred
depressed	gutsy	mellow
discouraged	happy	miserable
domineering	hateful	misunderstood
down	helpful	nervous
eager	helpless	noble
efficient	hesitant	nonchalant
elated	hopeless	nostalgic
embarrassed	humble	overwhelmed
encouraged	hurt	pained
energetic	impatient	passive
enthusiastic	important	peaceful
envious	impressed	peppy
excited	infatuated	playful
expectant	insecure	possessive
fascinated	insignificant	pressured
fearful	inspired	proud
fiendish	irked	pushed
foolish	irresistible	refreshed
forgetful	irritated	relieved
free	jealous	remorseful
frustrated	kind	resentful
full	lazy	satisfied
glad	let down	secure
gossipy	lonely	shy
grateful	lovable	skeptical
great	lovely	stupid

successful	timid	unhappy
sulky	tired	unloved
surprised	tranquil	unsure
suspicious	trapped	vulnerable
sympathetic	triumphant	warm
tempted	uncomfortable	weary
tender	understood	wonderful
threatened	uneasy	worried

As you read through the list, you probably recognized having felt all of the feelings at one time or another. Most people have. Yet very few people take into account the subtle differences in their feelings when they put a name to them. These subtleties, however, are important because when we have trouble differentiating irritation from anger or helplessness from depression, we run the risk of blowing challenging situations out of proportion. In addition, we become incapable of breaking down situations so that they're more manageable and easier to handle.

Practice differentiating between the subtle feelings you have about your ex. It takes time and patience to learn this skill, but it's well worth the results you'll achieve. Try these on for size:

I'm grateful that I'm not married to her anymore!

I'm impatient when my ex is late.

I felt trapped in my marriage.

I'm overjoyed with my new freedom.

I'm skeptical about any plans for reconciliation.

I no longer feel burdened.

I'm delighted that my ex isn't living here anymore.

Step 3: *Taking Responsibility for Your Feelings*

Once you become more skilled at differentiating your feelings, you'll find it easier to take responsibility for them. Taking responsibility means admitting that no one can make you feel a certain way. Your ex doesn't "make you" feel angry, frustrated, or disappointed; you simply feel that way. Another person may not feel angry, frustrated, or disappointed by her, even though your ex may have behaved in the exact same way with that person. Different people can feel differently as a result of the same action.

When you own or take responsibility for your feelings, you place yourself in a position of power and control. To do this, we suggest a two-step process: First, examine whether your initial feeling is masking a subtler one. For example, if you're furious because your ex didn't pick up your child on time and it ruined your plans, is it possible that your anger is masking a feeling of helplessness or frustration?

Second, once you've decided what you're feeling, put it into words. For example, let's say your anger is masking frustration that you have to change your plans when your ex is late. Instead of saying, "My ex makes me furious," take the subtler emotion (frustration) and say, "I feel frustrated that I had to change my plans."

In owning your subtle feelings, you've changed the situation from one where you had no control (because you can't change your ex or your feelings about him) to one that feels slightly more manageable (because you can make alternate arrangements to ensure that you don't have to change your plans no matter how your ex behaves).

THE BIGGER PICTURE

Identifying and owning your feelings are really part of a larger technique called the Think-Feel-Do cycle, first introduced by Dr. Michael Popkin. When you understand how this cycle works, you will be able to make even more changes that ease the tension and frustration of co-parenting with a jerk. Here's an explanation using Sarah and Ted from the previous chapter.

THE THINK-FEEL-DO CYCLE

Most people believe that when an event occurs, you feel a certain way.

Event

Feelings

For example, Ted might believe that Sarah's lateness causes him to feel enraged. He then might feel helpless as well, because he knows he can't change Sarah's actions. What Ted doesn't realize, however, is that an event does not cause us to feel a certain way. Events trigger thoughts and the thoughts trigger feelings.

Event

Thoughts

Feelings

Because the thoughts are so fleeting, people are often unaware of them. Thus people act solely upon their feelings. When they finally do act, this action causes the next event.

Next Event

Event

Action   Thoughts

Feelings

When your thoughts are negative, they trigger negative feelings, and when you act based on those feelings, you usually act in a negative manner, which causes the next event to be negative. On the other hand, when your thoughts are positive, they trigger positive feelings and the subsequent action is positive. For example, if the phone rings at a time when everything is going well, you optimistically wonder who is calling. Without looking at "Caller ID," you feel curious and excited about the possibility of speaking to a friend or hearing good news. But if you are anticipating bad news, the ring of the phone produces the thought that something's wrong. You feel a sense of dread, worry, and fright.

Your feelings then cause you to act. If you are excited, you run to the phone and eagerly pick it up, and if you're apprehensive, you slowly turn, perhaps pausing anxiously with your hand on the receiver until it rings one more time. When you finally pick up the phone, that action causes the next event in your life.

Here's a diagram of the Think-Feel-Do cycle using Ted and Sarah's original scenario:

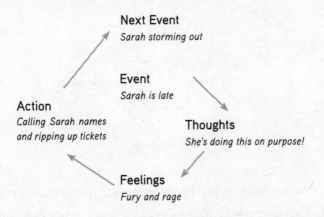

Next Event
Sarah storming out

Event
Sarah is late

Action
*Calling Sarah names
and ripping up tickets*

Thoughts
She's doing this on purpose!

Feelings
Fury and rage

When you understand that your feelings are triggered by what you think about an event and not by the event itself, you gain a measure of control. Although you cannot control the things (events) that happen to you, or change your feelings (after all, you feel the way you feel), you can change your thoughts. A change in thoughts often radically alters your feelings.

Let's start with Ted's thoughts about Sarah's tardiness. Some of the thoughts that came to mind were: *She's always late; I'm going to be late; Jason is ready to go. I hate her; She's ruined my life; I wish she would die.* These thoughts triggered Ted's anger, and his anger caused him to explode verbally, to act out by ripping up his concert tickets.

Changing Your Thoughts

In any Think-Feel-Do cycle, you are given two windows of opportunity that enable you to make a change in your thoughts.

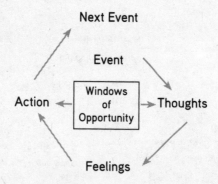

Many times, simply being aware that your thoughts exist is enough to alter your feelings in a cycle. Sometimes, however, it's necessary not only to be conscious of but also to actively rehearse alternate thoughts to keep negative ones from affecting you. The more you practice using alternate positive thoughts, the easier it becomes to see the positive side.

Let's see how it would look if Ted changed his thoughts about that evening through this window of opportunity. His thoughts could have been: *Well, better late than never. Maybe I can exchange the tickets for another night,* or *I'm disappointed, but I did get to spend some extra time with Jason and that's irreplaceable,* or *You know, I'd love to watch this show with him. Maybe she'll be willing to sit in her car until the show is over.*

If Ted had these thoughts when he opened the door, things would have been different. He wouldn't have called Sarah names and given her ammunition to start the cycle over.

CHANGING YOUR ACTIONS

Another window of opportunity that you can take advantage of involves changing what you do, no matter what feelings you have, by utilizing some proven communication techniques and replacing your normal, reactive communication in a cycle with some proactive communication. The remainder of this book is devoted to doing just that.

Step 4: *Breaking Down the Problem*

Once you have identified your feelings and owned them, looking at the Think-Feel-Do cycle in the process, you're then ready to break down complex issues into their more manageable components.

Let's take a look at a complicated problem that Mindy is having with her ex:

> When I found out John was having an affair, I told him to move out. He claimed he didn't have enough money for a security deposit on a new apartment, and then I found out, through our six-year-old son, Timmy, that John took his new girlfriend to the Bahamas for a long weekend. Well, I got so angry that I threw all his clothes into a pile and left them in the basement of our apartment building. When he finally showed up to get the rest of his things, he told me that he lost his job, so he's moving in with his sister. He insisted that Timmy spend the weekends with him, but I can't stand his sister. Or her kids. They're rude and even mean to Timmy at times. I finally gave in and said that Timmy could go for a weekend. And you know what my ex did? He told Timmy that if Mommy didn't let Daddy move back in, he'd have to move away and never see him again. Can you imagine how upset Timmy was? He came to me in tears! What am I going to do with this jerk? And when I attempt to talk to John, he just shrugs his shoulders and walks away. He thinks everything is fine, that I'm being unreasonable.

At first glance, Mindy's problem seems huge and unmanageable. One of the reasons it seems so challenging, however, is that it's not one but many problems. Mindy is feeling overwhelmed by a challenging situation. As many of us do when we feel over-whelmed, she has combined many small problems together to create one huge one that feels insurmountable. If you look closely, however, you'll see that the preceding example reflects more than eleven problems, some of which Mindy might be able to solve but many of which are not under her control. Problem (1) John had an affair. (2) John needs to find an apartment. (3) He doesn't have enough money for a security deposit. (4) John acts irresponsibly by taking off for the Bahamas. (5) John confides about his new girlfriend to Timmy. (6) Mindy acts immaturely by throwing out John's clothes. (7) John has lost his job. (8) John is moving in with his sister, whom Mindy can't stand. (9) John tells Timmy that he might have to move away and will never see him again, placing blame on Mindy. (10) Timmy is afraid he'll never see his dad again. (11) John denies responsibility for the problems.

WHAT EXACTLY IS THE PROBLEM HERE?

First things first: Mindy needs to separate her feelings from the facts so that she doesn't become reactive or paralyzed by her feelings. To begin, she's enraged about John's infidelity. And hurt. She's also sad about the end of her marriage and afraid of what the future will bring. She's insulted about being lied to about the money. She's frustrated that John won't talk about or admit to the problems that exist. She's uncomfortable that he confided about his new girlfriend to Timmy. She's heartbroken that her son was upset because John blamed her for the divorce and threatened to move away. She's also jealous because she doesn't have a boyfriend.

TO SOLVE OR NOT TO SOLVE

After you've isolated your feelings and before you set out to solve any problem, whether or not it involves your ex, you should ask yourself two questions: "What exactly is the problem?" and, "Is it worth my time and energy to solve it?"

To answer the first question, isolate the problem by looking at your Think-Feel-Do cycle and determine which feeling or feelings are the most intense. Then, "back up" and identify what you're thinking that's causing those feelings. After you've been through this process, then ask yourself if it's worth your time and energy to solve the problem.

ISOLATING THE PROBLEM

Let's look at how Mindy answers these questions. She wants to get her life back on track but is so upset with her ex that she doesn't know what to do next.

1. What feeling or feelings are the most intense? Mindy must first decide which of her feelings is the strongest. Since this may change from day to day or even from moment to moment, she should start with the most intense feeling that she's having right now. For example, she may be more worried about her financial situation tomorrow than she is today. Yesterday she may have been furious that John took his girlfriend to the Bahamas. Today she realizes that her concern about Timmy going to his aunt's house is steadily nagging at her and could be described as the most intense.

2. What are the thoughts causing that feeling? Upon reflection, Mindy recognizes these thoughts: *I can't stand John's sister. She always takes his side. Her children are rude and mean; I don't want Timmy to have his feelings hurt and I hate it that he's putting Timmy in this situation.*

3. Is it worth investing your time and energy to solve this problem? Although John has moved in with his sister, it is probably a temporary situation. Mindy should ask herself: If she intercedes at this point, will it prevent the development of a bigger problem? On the other hand, if she chooses to let it go, will the problem go away by itself? Further, could she empower Timmy to deal with his cousins if he has hurt or upset feelings and, in doing so, help him learn to deal with the uncooperative people whom he will inevitably come across in his life?

In examining these possibilities, she can either decide to put her foot down and refuse to let Timmy go or determine that in a few weeks the circumstances will probably be different. After a thorough examination of her feelings in relationship to both our questions and the Think-Feel-Do cycle, Mindy decided to let

John take Timmy to his sister's house for the weekend. When Mindy asked Timmy about it later, he reported that his weekend was "okay."

ACCEPTING TOLERABLE SITUATIONS

The last question, "Is it worth investing your time and energy to solve this problem?" is of the utmost importance. Many conflicts between you and your ex are fueled by anger, jealousy, and a desire for control. If you can take a deep breath and "don't sweat the small stuff," you will be able to move more smoothly forward on your own life's path.

The Serenity Prayer, written by Reinhold Niebuhr and widely adopted and used by members of twelve-step recovery programs, asks for the wisdom to know the difference between what you can change and what you can't. Maybe it will be helpful to you:

> *God grant me the serenity*
> *to accept the things I cannot change;*
> *courage to change the things I can;*
> *and wisdom to know the difference.*

Acceptance doesn't happen overnight. It's gradual. If you continue to expend your energy trying to change things that don't really matter in the long run or that are not within your sphere of influence, you'll wind up exhausted and frustrated, with no positive results to show for your effort.

While we spend the remainder of this book showing you how to change certain situations, it's important that you develop a certain level of acceptance about the things you cannot change. There is no doubt that raising a child with an uncooperative ex is a difficult task. Like we said in the beginning of this chapter, by accepting that it is difficult you make it easier. Knowing which problems aren't worth your while to solve frees you to move on, to have more fun, to feel better in general. And when you're feeling better, you can come up with more creative ways to solve the problems that do need your attention and effort.

When a problem can't be solved, an attitude of acceptance makes room in your mind and heart for solutions to the problems that do need to be solved.

3.

Who Tops the Problem Pyramid?

RESPONSIBILITY

In order to take responsibility for solving a problem, we must first recognize what responsibility means. It means knowing that the choices we make in our lives have consequences and it means being willing to accept that what happens to us is a direct result of those choices. Taking responsibility gives us power and control, because when we recognize the relationship between our choices and their consequences, then the next time we don't like a consequence we can make a different choice.

We often become bogged down in the problem-solving process because we come up with so many excuses for not solving the problem at all. Yet when we assume responsibility—when we, in effect, say, "I will be the one to do something about this situation," rather than saying, "Something should be done," or "Gee, I can't help it; I can't make a difference here"—we take the first step, which makes us more powerful and puts us in control.

Try the following exercise: Make a list of four or five things you can't do. For example, maybe you can't cook, speak a foreign language, or rollerblade. Say them slowly out loud: "I can't cook. I can't speak a foreign language. I can't rollerblade." See how you feel as you say them.

Now try it a different way. Instead of saying "can't," say "won't": "I won't cook. I won't speak a foreign language. I won't rollerblade." How do you feel now? Most people feel a little uncomfortable. There's power in the word "won't," and when you say it you claim control and responsibility for not doing those things.

Most people upon trying this exercise protest, "It's not that I *won't* do those things, it's that I just *can't*. I simply don't have the time. I mean, I'd love to learn a foreign language and rollerblade, but I've got other priorities."

Your priorities are the key. You may choose not to make learning a foreign language or rollerblading a priority and choose other priorities instead—and that's okay. But you're not a victim of some unseen force and consequently "can't" do them. When you say "won't," you recognize your ability to change priorities if you so choose or to understand your reasons for not changing them. By taking responsibility, you are able to control your life, instead of feeling that you're a victim of circumstances.

CONTRIBUTING TO THE SOLUTION

It's important to admit that we sometimes have a tendency to contribute to the problem rather than to the solution. Looking at your piece in the custody puzzle includes examining your own actions, reactions, and motivations for behaving the way you do. When trying to solve problems with your ex, ask yourself if you are contributing to the problem. One mother admitted to chugging a beer before she called her ex so that she could "get angry" and "be more effective" with him. Although alcohol is socially and legally acceptable from the White House to the Vatican, it is a mood-altering drug, and a depressant at that. Chugging a beer or even simply getting angry on purpose to feel more effective contributes to the problem rather than to the solution.

Sometimes your contribution to the problem involves covering for your ex. One father couldn't figure out why his wife couldn't manage her money and refused to see that he constantly bailed her out of financial holes, which enabled her to remain irresponsible.

Other times, your contribution to the problem involves engaging in avoidance techniques. These enable you to avoid responsibility for coming up with a solution to the problem. At the same time they can allow the problem to continue or become worse. The ones to watch for include justifying your actions, making assumptions, engaging in deliberate manipulation, projecting the worst, and placing blame. Recognizing these behaviors in yourself takes you one more step down the road to having a more successful custody relationship. Here are some examples:

JUSTIFYING YOUR ACTIONS

Our son is having a hard time in school and complains of headaches a lot, especially on Monday mornings. I have always believed that in addition to sick days we need mental health days, so I don't really have a problem with letting my son stay home if he's upset. Recently, though, the school confronted me about his absences. I told them that he was going through a hard time because of the divorce and it seemed sensible to keep him home. I said that we were doing things that were educational like going to the zoo and watching historical movies I'd rented. I felt perfectly justified until they pointed out that he'd been absent four of the last five Mondays. I guess I didn't realize it had been that many days!

This mom felt, in her own words, "justified" in keeping her son home from school because he was having a hard time with the divorce and because they were doing "educational" things. But in justifying her actions she was also effectively avoiding the real issue: Her son was having a hard time with the divorce and was missing a lot of school because of it. Once the school helped her see that she was avoiding responsibility and contributing to the problem by justifying her actions, she was able to get the help for her son that he needed in the first place.

MAKING ASSUMPTIONS

I'm sure the only reason my ex wants to see Nick on Saturdays instead of Sundays is because she wants to stay overnight at her boyfriend's on Saturdays.

By assuming that his ex's ulterior motive involves her own selfish pleasure, this father adds an element to the problem that might not be present. For example, would he feel differently if he found out that rather than wanting to spend time with her boyfriend, his ex wants to see Nick on Saturdays because her work schedule has changed and she now has to work on Sundays? When we make assumptions, we contribute to the complexity rather than the simplicity of a problem, making it more difficult to solve.

ENGAGING IN DELIBERATE MANIPULATION

I don't want my ex to go to the hockey awards dinner with us so I'm telling him that we're not going, either. Then we'll just change our minds at the last minute and go.

You've heard Sir Walter Scott's "0, what a tangled web we weave, when first we practice to deceive." Being manipulative is dishonest and immature. We often end up having to make up more lies to cover for inconsistencies in our original manipulation. In addition, it sets a terrible example for our children. While it may solve your initial problem, the tangled web that grows from such dishonesty is more trouble than it's worth.

PROJECTING THE WORST

I just know that whatever toys I send with the kids on the weekend will end up coming back broken or with missing pieces.

None of us are fortune-tellers, and when we pretend that we are and look into our imaginary crystal ball we usually only see the negative. Projecting into the future about what "might" or "could" happen causes us to creatively suffer in the present. Don't add to your problems by projecting the worst. A problem isn't a problem until it actually happens.

PLACING BLAME

Tommy had been having trouble sleeping, and I just knew it was because his father let him play violent video games. When he came home after a weekend there, it would take him three or four days to settle back down and be able to sleep again. I was furious with his father and blaming him was easy. But when Tommy's sleeping behavior got worse, I sought professional help, basically so I could have ammunition against his father. The counselor gently suggested that maybe Tommy was having trouble making the transition from his father's house back to the routine at my house, and that maybe the games they played weren't the real cause of his sleep problem. When she and I explored that possibility with Tommy together, it turned out that she was right. And we uncovered a whole lot more about the divorce that was bothering him. Once things were out in the open, and we worked on them a bit, Tommy went back to sleeping just fine.

Blaming another person for a problem often keeps us from examining the different possibilities that may underlie the issue. Blame is an effective way of putting on dark shades and looking at a problem from only one point of view. If you often hear yourself saying things like, "I didn't say that," "You didn't tell me that," "You never said that," you may need to take a look at the problem from a different perspective. Draw your Think-Feel-Do cycle. What are your feelings, your thoughts? What action did you take that might have produced a negative event? We're not suggesting that your ex is blame free or that he is telling you everything he claims or even that he is remembering everything you have told him. We're suggesting that you honestly look at the ways you might be contributing to the problem instead of to the solution. Once you've taken this step, you'll find that the problem becomes much simpler and therefore easier to handle.

ALLOWING GUILT

Another way we subconsciously avoid taking action in solving problems is by allowing guilt, the "shoulds" and "shouldn'ts" in our lives, to bring us to a standstill. Subconsciously, we may believe that if we feel guilty enough, it will absolve us from doing anything about it. A simple grammatical shift, however, can change us from a guilty victim to an effective and assertive problem solver and move us forward. To make this shift, simply substitute the word "could" for "should" and see the difference it makes in clarifying the choices you have as well as the consequences of those choices.

"I *should* stay inside this weekend and clean out all the stuff my ex didn't take with her when she left" sounds like you have no choice in the matter. "I *could* stay in this weekend and clean out all the stuff my ex didn't take with her when she left" sounds as if it's one of many choices you might make in deciding how to spend your weekend. "I could make a bonfire with her things. I could invite my friends over to watch me light it. We could toast marshmallows!" There's more power in "could" because it assumes you have options.

Guilt also rears its ugly head because of the perception we have of the way things "should" be. Many times media-fabricated role models (most sitcom moms and dads for example) persuade us to believe that we can be supermen and superwomen. Then when we don't want to be or do everything, we feel guilty. Likewise, we sometimes believe that we not only *can* do everything, but we must also *want* to do everything. When our feelings run counter to this pressure, guilt ensues.

Guilt is helpful only when it keeps us acting in line with our beliefs and morals. Otherwise, it creates needless suffering. In addition, because it implies a deep-seated belief that we've done something "wrong," it eats away at our self-esteem and makes it less likely that we will see our future choices and options and be confident about acting on them.

Practice switching the word "could" for the word "should" in your vocabulary and see what options and choices it opens up for you. Recognizing these options and claiming responsibility for your choices gives you power. Sometimes that power may scare you or you may feel a little uncomfortable with it because you're not used to it, but wouldn't it be nice, in situations with your ex, to feel like you're in control?

CLAIMING POWER

It may take some time for you to get used to catching yourself and changing your thoughts, so we've provided some common ways many people avoid responsibility, and we've made some suggestions on how to reword those old, powerless choices. By identifying when you use these (even if at first you don't recognize them until days after you've said them), you'll be on the road to claiming power and taking responsibility for the choices you make.

Old: "I can't/couldn't [go to dinner, get my career going, etc.] because [my child-care responsibilities are too burdensome]."
New: "I'm choosing not to [go to dinner, get my career going, etc.] because I've chosen to [put my efforts into raising a healthy daughter/son]."

Old: "Why didn't you tell me [Suzy's tuition was due, spring break was coming up, the soccer game is on Friday]?"

New: "I didn't [look up the tuition payment schedule, the spring break dates, the soccer schedule]."

Old: "You make me [so angry, look bad in front of the other parents]."

New: "I feel [so angry, concerned that I look bad in front of the other parents]."

Old: "If only I didn't have to deal with [my ex, that 'jerk'], then I'd be able to get things under control."

New: "It's unfortunate that I have to deal with [my ex, that 'jerk'], but I'm working to get things under control."

Old: "I should [clean the house this weekend], but I know I'll never get around to it."

New: "I could [clean the house this weekend], but I may choose to [go to the gym] instead."

Old: "Well, what do you expect from me? I can't help it; I'm going through a difficult time right now."

New: "I'm going through a difficult time right now. I'm trying my best. At least I got nominated for the Pulitzer Prize. Maybe next time I'll win it." ☺

THE FLIP SIDE OF THE COIN: TAKING TOO MUCH RESPONSIBILITY

Once you understand that taking responsibility for your choices gives you control and you accept that the choices you've made have consequences, you'll be able to make better choices in the future. In addition, learning to phrase your communication without blaming, avoiding, or denying responsibility allows you to begin to identify situations in which you are responsible and distinguish them from the situations in which you aren't responsible.

Now, fair warning: Because taking responsibility gives you control, there can be a temptation to take on too much responsibility. Many people believe that they have to fix everything and everyone, because if they don't, no one else will. These people often take on responsibilities that don't belong to them, such as responsibility for someone else's feelings or problems. The person who takes too much responsibility often feels overwhelmed and unappreciated, while the person who takes too little responsibility feels controlled and suffocated. When this happens, it complicates situations so vastly that it's difficult even to begin working out a solution to the problem. To help you determine whether or not you are taking on problems that don't actually require your time and energy to solve, we've included a technique here called the problem pyramid, which allows you to sort out what you have control over and what you do not.

THE PROBLEM PYRAMID

People often spend a great deal of time spinning their wheels, trying to solve problems that don't belong to them. For example, when a child feels afraid at night because he thinks there are "monsters" under the bed, many parents set out to solve that problem. They say things like, "Well, let's look under the bed; then you'll see there are no monsters," or they invent a special "monster spray" and go to great lengths to spray the room so the monsters will leave. But do the monsters go away? Not likely.

The challenge lies in determining to whom the problem belongs. A monster under the bed is actually not the parent's problem; it's the child's. And because the problem belongs to the child, the solution for solving the problem also belongs to the child. We're not suggesting that you abandon a frightened child, but rather that you use supportive techniques that empower your child to come up with a solution himself. (These techniques are described in detail in chapter 7, "When Your Child Tops the Problem Pyramid.")

If you fail to recognize that problems like these belong to your child, you will spend a great deal of time, energy, and frustration trying valiantly to help by taking on the problem yourself.

Figuring out to whom a problem belongs in a particular situation does not permit you to wash your hands of it, blame someone else, or rush in and save the day. Instead it allows you to decide which course of action to take.

The following problem pyramid will help you sort out who really needs to be taking responsibility for solving a particular problem. Once you know who is responsible, you can decide the most effective way to promote a solution. Read the pyramid from bottom to top.

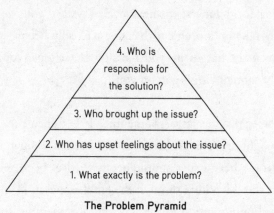

4. Who is responsible for the solution?

3. Who brought up the issue?

2. Who has upset feelings about the issue?

1. What exactly is the problem?

The Problem Pyramid

Now let's break it down and discover how this simple formula can enable you to effectively solve a problem like this one: Your ex barges into your home without knocking when she picks up your child.

1. What exactly is the problem? By looking at your feelings and identifying your thoughts in the Think-Feel-Do cycle, you can break a big problem down into its individual components and look at them separately. Your thoughts in the case of the ex who barges in may be that your ex doesn't live here anymore and has no right to just walk in. You may feel exposed and intruded upon.

2. Who has upset feelings about the issue? List all parties whose feelings are upset. Note that we don't say "all parties who have feelings about the issue." This level is specifically for negative feelings. Because more than one name can go on this level, it's important to look at the next level as well. If you stop here, you may take on a problem that doesn't really belong to you. When your ex barges in, you have upset feelings. Your ex is perfectly content barging in on you.

3. Who brought up the issue? Sometimes it is difficult to decide who brought up the issue because it can seem as though two or more people have issues simultaneously. Also, because you're the one who is working through the problem pyramid and who is focused on a solution to the problem, it sometimes seems as though you're always the only one raising an issue. Keep in mind that only one person can bring up an issue at a time and it's usually (although not always) the person who verbalized it first. When your ex is happily barging in, she won't bring this up to you because it's not an issue to her. You have an issue with it.

4. Who is responsible for the solution? It is the combination of levels 2 and 3 that determines who is responsible for implementing a solution to the problem. If you have upset feelings and you're also bringing the issue up as a problem, then your name will appear on both level 2 and 3 and, thus, also on level 4.

4a. Conversely, if your ex has upset feelings and has brought up the issue (whether or not she believes it is a problem), then your ex's name belongs on levels 2, 3, and 4.

4b. It is also possible that your child may have upset feelings and be bringing up the issue, and then his or her name will appear on levels 2, 3, and therefore 4 of the problem pyramid.

It's unlikely that the names on levels 2 and 3 will be different, because people who are content with a situation rarely bring it up as an issue (like the ex who barges in). It is, however, theoretically possible to have different names on these levels. In this case, level 3 alone determines who tops the problem pyramid.

It's important to note that the person whose name appears on level 4 will not necessarily be motivated to find a solution to the problem himself. But your next action will be directed by the name that appears here. If your name appears here, you'll use the techniques in chapter 4, "When You Top the Problem Pyramid." If your ex's name appears here, you'll use the techniques in chapter 9, "When Your Ex Tops the Problem Pyramid." And if your child's name appears here, you'll go to chapter 7, "When Your Child Tops the Problem Pyramid." (But don't go there now! Keep reading from here!)

COMMON PROBLEMS AND IDENTIFYING WHO TOPS THEM

To help you identify who tops the problem, look at the following scenarios. We've started you off with fairly simple problems for the sake of clarity and to help you learn the technique more easily.

"My ex doesn't pack my son's religion school homework on the weekends I see him."
Who has upset feelings? You.
Who raised the issue? You.
Who tops the pyramid? You.

"Daddy makes me go to bed at eight on Saturday nights."
Who has upset feelings? The child.
Who raised the issue? The child.
Who tops the pyramid? The child.

"My ex called me at 2:00 A.M. because our son was running a one hundred–degree fever."
Who has upset feelings? Your ex (and you, for being awakened).
Who raised the issue? Your ex.
Who tops the pyramid? Your ex.

My ex reads the emails I send to my son.
Who has upset feelings? You (and maybe your child).

Who raised the issue? You (and maybe your child).
Who tops the pyramid? You (and maybe your child).

Now let's take a more complex situation. Let's say that nine-year-old Amy calls her mom, Jane, at seven thirty on a Saturday night, crying because her dad won't let her watch television and has told her that she must go to bed in a half hour:

I was just about to leave to see a movie when the phone rang. It was Amy, crying hysterically. She was begging to come home because her dad wanted her to go to bed and wouldn't let her watch her favorite TV show. Why does he have to put her to bed so early? Anyway, Amy kept crying and crying. By the time she calmed down, it was too late for my movie. I was angry and exhausted and my night was shot!

Who tops this problem pyramid? At first glance, most people would automatically assume that Mom has a problem because she has to miss her movie. In addition, it's clear that Mom has taken sides with Amy. She, too, feels that the bedtime is ridiculous, and when Mom's feelings are involved and her plans are ruined, she's very likely to assume that this problem is hers and go about solving it. The challenge here is that if Mom decides it's her problem and takes it up with her ex, tempers are likely to rise and Mom may end up wasting a lot of time and energy spinning her wheels. Let's work through the problem pyramid and see who really needs to solve this problem:

1. *What exactly is the problem?* Amy isn't having a good time at her dad's, so she called Mom, crying. Mom's plans to go out are now ruined because she has to spend time calming Amy down.

2. *Who has upset feelings about the issue?* Amy is upset because bedtime is too early; Mom is upset that her plans are ruined.

3. *Who brought up the issue?* Amy. (If Amy hadn't called Mom, Mom wouldn't have an issue.)

4. *Who tops the problem pyramid?* Amy! Because Amy's name appears on the second two levels of the pyramid, the most effective route for Mom to take will involve supporting Amy in solving her own problem. When Mom empowers Amy to deal directly with her dad, she can avoid engaging in a battle with her ex over the rules in his house, where he has the final authority. By allowing Amy to deal directly with her dad, Mom will help Amy feel more confident and more in control and she will be less likely to need her mom's help in the future. Subsequently, Jane will achieve her Saturday nights without phone calls from Amy or conflicts with Amy's dad.

In cases where your child has a problem, it's important to remember that even though you're divorced, the bottom line is that you're still a parent, and as such you are responsible for listening to your child when he has a problem even if it affects your plans. We understand that this can be a time-consuming and frustrating process, but if you take the time to do this, it will empower your child to solve his own problems and can actually save you time in the future.

Try this one: "My ex-wife constantly rearranges visitation whenever our son is even slightly ill. I think her new husband is afraid of getting sick and having to miss work at his big-shot job."

Who has upset feelings? The new husband and you.
Who brought up the issue? The new husband.
Who tops the problem pyramid? The new husband.

Now try the next few on your own. Don't get hung up on what the solution will be; simply figure out who tops the pyramid.

1. My daughter is taking antibiotics and my ex never remembers to give her the medicine at the right time.
2. Every few months my ex calls and tells me his whole financial situation, and how terrible things are. I'm sure he's trying to get me to reduce what I receive in child support.
3. My ex thinks it's perfectly okay for our daughter to skip her softball practice on the weekends she's with him.
4. My ex screams at me about our daughter's grades. I think she's doing fine, considering the stress she's under.

5. My daughter says, "I hate Daddy's new wife. She makes me wash the dishes and clean the whole house. I'm never going there again!"
6. My ex always gives our son bigger presents than I can afford.
7. My son just exclaimed, "Mommy is so mean! She makes me walk home from school every day."
8. Every time my husband chats with the kids on Skype, I feel like he's snooping and trying to see if I've changed anything in the house.

When you've figured out who tops the problem pyramid, you'll know who is responsible for implementing the solution to each of these problems. Remember that no matter who tops the problem pyramid, you'll still take steps to promote the solution. The pyramid simply directs your actions.

Answers to Who Tops the Problem Pyramid:

1. You
2. Your ex
3. You
4. Your ex
5. Your child
6. You
7. Your child
8. You

4.

When You Top the Problem Pyramid

PICK YOUR BATTLES

One of the most important components of successful conflict resolution is learning to pick your battles. Before you raise an issue with your ex, think it through carefully and ask yourself if it's really important. An ex who chooses to battle about every single thing runs the risk of being dismissed out-of-hand, with an, "Ugghh, she's always on about something," and ignored. While you certainly need to stand up for what you truly believe in, sometimes it really doesn't matter if your child wears her mittens, feasts on junk food one day a week, or gets that bath tonight or tomorrow night. Sometimes, it's more effective to let it go or take care of things yourself.

Jake spends Tuesday nights with his dad. When I clean out his lunch box on Wednesdays, I find candy wrappers, cookie crumbs, and chips. I don't even think his dad packs a sandwich, just junk. I want Jake to have a healthier lunch, but I decided it really wouldn't get me anywhere to bring it up with his dad. So now I either drop Jake's lunch off at his school on Wednesdays or pack him a healthy lunch the night before and send it with him. Or I just let it go for one day.

Rather than engaging in a battle with her ex, this mom decided that it was simply easier to circumvent the problem by taking action herself. There are many situations like this, as well as situations that might call for letting go and not doing anything. Still, other problems will require that you do go that "extra mile" and intervene because it's just too important not to do so.

In any case where you feel that you need to intercede, it's best to set yourself up for success by formulating a plan of action.

CREATE A PLAN OF ACTION

Have you ever been on a car trip where you didn't need to arrive anywhere at a specific time? On this trip, you could drive until you got tired, see the sights along the way, stop at a motel when it seemed convenient, and continue driving whenever you woke up the next morning. It's a wonderful way to travel. There's no pressure and no stress. But would you travel this way if you had to make a business meeting? Of course not. It's inefficient and imprecise, and you would probably miss the meeting if you didn't sit down ahead of time and make a plan.

Like taking a car trip to a business meeting, topping the

problem pyramid means that you must plan a trip (in this case a communication trip) that will get you where you want to go in the shortest amount of time. Developing a plan of action means creating a blueprint of the communication you are about to have with your ex.

This plan or blueprint should include several pieces of information: (1) when and where you will speak with your ex, (2) how you can disengage if things become hostile, (3) what your "I" statement and positive assertion will be, and (4) what actions you will take if the "I" statement isn't heeded. We'll explain "I" statements and positive assertions in the next few pages.

DECIDE WHEN AND WHERE TO SPEAK TO YOUR EX

While the techniques we describe can be used on the spur of the moment (and are often extremely effective when applied this way), it is always better to set up a time and place to speak to your ex if you can. Think back to the metaphor of going on a business trip: If you had to suddenly drop everything and leave, you might forget to pack something essential like your underwear. Granted, you still might make it to the meeting on time and handle yourself well, but you'd probably feel vulnerable and uncomfortable.

When you make an appointment with your ex to discuss an important issue, you are making a commitment to give her your undivided attention and you're requesting the same from her. This is an act of respect that sets the stage for problem solving. It gives both of you time to think through your positions on the given subject, to prepare your arguments logically—not emotionally—and to feel comfortable and informed.

When you don't arrange a time in advance, you invite your ex to discount or argue with you because you're catching him off-guard. You may evoke an emotional response rather than a logical one. He may be angry about something totally unrelated to your issue and displace that anger onto you. In many cases, the old adage "timing is everything" is true. Look at what Jillian had to say about an exchange with her ex, Ben:

I met this guy, Chris, and he asked me out for Friday. I hadn't been on a date in months and I was really excited. Plus, my daughter, Diana, was staying with her father for the weekend. Well, right when I got home on Friday I got a text message from Chris saying that something had come up and he couldn't keep our date. I was devastated—disappointed that I wasn't going out and angry that he hadn't called to speak to me in person. In the middle of all this, my ex rings the doorbell and the first words out of his mouth are, "Why does Diana have to go to the dentist twice a year? Isn't once a year enough for a checkup? And did you have to pick the most expensive dentist in town? There must be someone cheaper!" As he went on and on and on about the dentist, I lost it. I slammed the door in his face. Diana heard us shouting and got all upset. What can I say? I guess I made a mess out of everything—again.

Ben made the mistake of trying to discuss an important issue without making an appointment. If he had called ahead and said, "Listen, I really need to talk to you about Diana's dental bills. Is this a good time?" Jillian could have said, "No, it isn't. I'm busy with something right now. How about tomorrow morning around ten?" or, "Sure, now is as good a time as any."

When making an appointment with your ex, no matter which of you is raising the issue, it's always a good idea to set a time within the next forty-eight hours and be prompt about keeping that appointment.

FIND A NEUTRAL TERRITORY

Once you make an appointment, you need a place to meet. It's best to choose a neutral setting—someplace outside of either of your offices or homes. This ensures that the children aren't running around or listening. Leave plenty of time to get there so you don't feel pressured by outside responsibilities.

Martha called and said she wanted to talk about the visitation arrangements. I told her that I couldn't talk now but that tonight would be good. She said fine and then suggested we meet at her place. When she mentioned her place, which used to be "our" place, I felt the hairs on my neck stand up.

Meeting on your ex's territory puts you at a disadvantage, especially if it used to be your home, too. Being there may distract you. You might find yourself looking around to see what has changed and what hasn't. In addition, it's typical for old surroundings to trigger old patterns of behavior.

Similarly, going to your ex's office places you in an unbalanced position. It's common to consider someone sitting behind a desk as an authority figure. If your ex assumes that position, your argument or issue may be substantially weakened because of this dynamic. Your feelings of discomfort could affect your level of confidence. Your ex may be emboldened and overly aggressive as well, due to his familiar surroundings. If you can't discuss something on the phone, go to a coffee shop, museum, department store, or park bench.

REFRAME YOUR RELATIONSHIP: THIS ISN'T WAR, IT'S BUSINESS

Old patterns of behavior are difficult to break. Before you go into a meeting with your ex, it's helpful to imagine your relationship with him or her as a business relationship rather than a personal one. Consider your children your most valuable assets and your ex a business partner or client with whom you must work in order to keep those assets intact. As you begin your meeting, ask yourself, *If this were a client I was trying to sell something to or if it were a million-dollar account that I wanted to secure, how would I behave?*

Most businesspeople don't engage in a verbally abusive war with each other. Even clients who misunderstand and resist you are treated with kid gloves, especially if they have an account you want.

It's equally important to keep other feelings, especially those of resentment and anger, out of the negotiation process with your ex. Just as you wouldn't share that you're feeling fat, ugly, and depressed with a client or tell her that you've just met the love of your life and you've never been happier, these thoughts and feelings should be kept to yourself and not shared with your ex.

Keep your focus on your assets (your children) and the business at hand. As you would with a client, actively watch for opportunities where you can admit that your ex has a good idea. This is known as win-win negotiating. In business, it helps clients feel listened to and important. While it may be more difficult to do with your ex, it will have the same effect:

> My ex called up with a suggestion for the holidays. I've realized that I'm prejudiced about everything he says these days. So I initiated this experiment: I pretended that it was a mother from my kids' school calling with the same suggestion. And you know what? It didn't sound so stupid coming from her.

Finally, as in any good business relationship, be honest and prepared to deliver what you promise. If you know you can't be flexible on Sunday, don't say that you can be. If you know that you're going to let your daughter go on that overnight birthday party, don't lie and tell your ex that you're not.

KNOW WHAT YOU WANT FROM YOUR EX

Knowing what you want before you start your meeting, just as you would in business, will keep you focused and often help you achieve your desired outcome:

> My ex's checks kept bouncing and my bank was on my case about it. My ex claimed that it was his bank's fault. I decided before our meeting that I wanted a letter of apology from his bank to my bank, and when my ex said, "Fine," I was amazed!

USE "I" STATEMENTS TO COMMUNICATE

An "I" statement is a simple sentence of which you are the subject. "I" statements begin with the word "I" and allow you to communicate your thoughts, feelings, and desires without blaming someone else: "I feel suspicious about this," "I feel uneasy," and "I am fine with this" are all examples of "I" statements.

When you top the problem pyramid and have a situation that you would like to change, we recommend that you formulate your communication using an "I" statement. In fact, whether you top the pyramid or not, the ability to speak in "I" statements is a flexible communication skill that is effective in all conversations, whether they be with your ex-spouse, children, parents, boss, or employees. We'll explain why "I" statements are so effective momentarily.

To fully understand "I" statements, it's helpful first to contrast them with "you" statements. "You" statements blame the other person for a situation, are accusatory in tone, and trigger defensiveness.

Let's look at a few "you" statements:

"You're never on time."

"If you don't listen to me, I'm taking you back to court."

"Why do you have to be so argumentative?"

"You" statements have the other person as their subject and are a form of verbal attack. More often than not, they trigger a defensive reaction and a negative Think-Feel-Do cycle.

Conversely, in an "I" statement the speaker, rather than the other person, is the subject of the sentence. Here's how they would sound, given the same subject matter as before:

"I'm frustrated that it's past the time we agreed upon."

"I feel interrupted and unheard."

"I don't want to argue."

WHY "I" STATEMENTS ARE EFFECTIVE

"I" statements are non-threatening and inherently respectful. If you keep your tone of voice neutral, it's difficult to argue with them. Let's face it, most people are unlikely to respond to "I feel frustrated" with "No, you don't" or to "I don't want to argue" with "Yes, you do."

In addition, it's difficult to respond defensively to "I" statements. While "you" statements cause people to feel that they are being attacked or threatened in some way, "I" statements simply put your thoughts and feelings out on the table. Because the person to whom you're speaking doesn't feel as though she has to defend herself or protect her self-esteem, she's likely to respond more favorably.

Another reason "I" statements work so well is because they allow you to remain calm. By memorizing the formula "I feel ___," "I think ___," "I would like ___," much like an actor memorizes lines, you relieve yourself of the pressure to improvise.

Even though this new way of speaking may not come naturally at first, with practice you will be able to make it part of your speech pattern. And while your ex may never be able to communicate in this same manner, if at least one person uses these techniques in an exchange, explosions are often avoided.

TONE OF VOICE AND BODY LANGUAGE

In the preceding section, we alluded to using a neutral tone of voice when communicating with "I" statements. The role of tone, as well as that of body language, should not be underestimated. In his studies, Dr. Albert Mehrabian, of UCLA, discovered that there are three main components to communication: words, tone of voice, and body language. He found that if tone of voice or facial expression disagrees with the words a person is using, the listener will believe the non-verbal cues and not the words.

Put in context, if you say, "I feel disappointed," but your tone of voice is angry and menacing, it's likely the other person will hear something more along the lines of what you might like to say: "You're a total jerk and I want to kill you right now!" Similarly, if "I don't want to argue" is said with an argumentative tone of voice, the other person will hear that combative tone and respond by arguing.

Body language and eye contact are also important. If you avert your eyes, hunch your shoulders, and shuffle your feet when you use an "I" statement, you turn power over to your ex. It's important to have a confident body posture in order to get your point across.

POSITIVE ASSERTIONS DISARM YOUR OPPONENT

"I" statements are a powerful tool when used in their simplest form, as we've outlined previously. They can be made even more effective when you add a positive assertion afterward. A positive assertion tells the other person what you want to have happen next or specifically what you want him to do differently:

"I'm frustrated that it's past the time we agreed upon." ("I" statement) "Please be on time." (positive assertion)

"I feel interrupted and unheard." ("I" statement) "Please listen to what I have to say, then I'll be happy to listen to you." (positive assertion)

"I don't want to argue." ("I" statement) "I'd like to take a break from talking about this until we both cool off." (positive assertion)

POSITIVE VERSUS NEGATIVE ASSERTIONS

When choosing the words in your positive assertion, it's best to say what you *do* want, rather than what you *don't*. For example, "please watch your language" is more powerful than "please don't swear." Likewise, "please be on time" rather than "please don't be late" helps to create a positive expectation for the other person.

When you phrase things negatively—"don't do this," "stop doing that"—you essentially send the message to the other person that you expect him to do the "wrong" thing. People often fail to hear the words "don't" and "stop" in a sentence and hear only what follows. If you say, "Don't swear at me," what they hear is "Swear at me." In addition, they can become "stuck" on the word "don't" and begin thinking, *Don't you dare tell me what to do!* This rise in defensiveness not only makes them miss your message but also often results in them lashing out at you.

INTER-GENDER COMMUNICATION

Much has been written about the differences in the communication styles of the genders. John Gray's *Men Are from*

Mars, Women Are from Venus and Deborah Tannen's *You Just Don't Understand* provide good examples of how difficult inter-gender communication can be. We're not saying the Y chromosome has either damaged or enlightened one special area of the brain, arguing nature versus nurture, or playing on stereotypes; we're just making the point that most men communicate differently from most women.

Women have a tendency to be tuned into and sensitive to feelings. They respond well when another person talks about how he or she feels. Men, on the other hand, prefer to know where they stand. They don't want a lot of "emoting" going on. In general, they respond more positively if they're told what action you would like them to take.

The "I" statement, combined with a positive assertion, appeals to both genders. When used by a man, it reminds him to include his feelings—thus his ex-wife is more likely to hear what he has to say, because in all likelihood she responds well to hearing and talking about feelings. Similarly, when used by a woman, it reminds her to be specific about what she'd like her ex-husband to do about the situation, which is usually all he wants to know anyway.

Depending upon which gender you're speaking to, you can adjust the basic formula to be even more effective. When speaking to a man, put the positive assertion first and follow it with the "I" statement: "I would like you to use more respectful language in my presence. I feel angry when I hear swearing." When speaking to a woman, tell her what you feel first: "I feel angry when you swear at me. Please use more respectful language in my presence."

ELIMINATE "ALWAYS" AND "NEVER"

When using "I" statements and positive assertions, it's important to eliminate the words "always" and "never." Things are rarely "always" or "never" true, and saying they are invariably inflames the listener. It's important to deal with each situation as if it were isolated from all others, keep it in the present, and refrain from dredging up the past. Granted, half of our anger and frustration occurs from repeated offenses, but if you can focus on what's happening right now, you'll more likely be able to effect a change.

Take a look at the following, which is filled with both "you" statements as well as the words "always" and "never":

You're always late and you've made me late again. You never consider my schedule. You never budget your time. Why are you always so inconsiderate?

Now take a look at this second statement:

I'm angry because I missed my movie tonight. Please arrive earlier next week.

It's easy to see how the first statement will trigger defensiveness and create an argument over whether the person is actually "always" late or not. In contrast, the person delivering the second message remains in control by staying in the present and owning his feelings.

Make no mistake, however. You can easily ruin "I" statements and positive assertions by inserting the words "never" and "always." Take a look at this third statement:

I'm angry because you never arrive on time. I always wind up having to cancel my plans. Please be on time from now on.

MAKE YOUR COMMUNICATION EFFECTIVE

When you begin using "I" statements and positive assertions, you may have a tendency simply to take your "old" style of communication and fit it into the form. For example:

I'm furious because you're being such an idiot.

Please, won't you finally get your act together and be on time?

I'm enraged with your constant lack of responsibility. Please step up to the plate for once in your life.

When you call the other person names or use intense feeling words such as "furious" and "enraged," your ex is likely to react defensively and intensely. To be as effective as possible, it's important to drop the name-calling and take a closer look at the strong emotion you're having or conveying. It's likely that your strong feelings are actually masking one of the subtler emotions we talked about in chapter 2. When an "I" statement is based on the underlying instead of the masking emotion, it comes closer to expressing our true thoughts.

Let's take a look at some typical communication and define the masking emotion that will, most likely, drive us to act. Then we'll determine the possible underlying emotion and formulate our "I" statement and positive assertion based on that.

> **Old:** *"You're an idiot for forgetting Sasha's umbrella. Don't you ever think before you act?"*
> **Masking emotion:** Anger
> **Underlying emotion:** Worry about Sasha's health
>
> **New:** *"I feel worried for Sasha's health when she gets wet from the rain. Please bring her umbrella the next time it's raining."*

> **Old:** *"I can't believe you forgot Mark's birthday again. It doesn't take a rocket scientist to remember these things, you know!"*
> **Masking emotion:** Disgust (communicated with sarcasm)
> **Underlying emotion:** Disappointment
>
> **New:** *"I'm disappointed that you forgot Mark's birthday. Please set a reminder on your BlackBerry for next year."*

Old: *"I can't believe you didn't come to Amanda's school play. You are so inconsiderate."*
Masking emotion: Disbelief
Underlying emotion: Sadness

New: *"I'm sad that you missed Amanda's play. She's having a piano recital next week and I'd like you to come to that."*

Old: *"I'm not bringing Lizzy over to your house, you jerk. Why can't you get off your butt for a change and come get her?"*
Masking emotion: Outrage
Underlying emotion: Frustration

New: *"I'm frustrated at having to bring Lizzy to your house. I'd like to work out a different schedule."*

Once you practice looking for the underlying emotion, it will begin to feel more comfortable to you. Each time you have an intense emotion, make the assumption that it's masking something else and stop yourself from saying anything until you have a more descriptive feeling word to use.

PRACTICE MAKES PERFECT

Start practicing "I" statements and positive assertions today. Try them on your children:

I feel annoyed by the clothes on the bathroom floor. Please put them in the laundry basket.

Next try your friend:

I'm feeling sad because I'm not dating anyone right now. Could we please refrain from talking about romantic relationships for a while and talk instead about getting together this weekend?

Now try some on your ex:

I feel frustrated when Jen arrives at my house without her hat and gloves. Please remember to pack them, even if the weather isn't cold.

I feel inconvenienced when I don't know your plans for Hannah until Saturday morning. Please pick her up on Saturdays by eleven.

I feel concerned about David's feelings when he's left out of a party at your house that includes your other kids. Please invite him next time.

Now try one in a different gender form. Be conscious to use feeling words other than anger.

Speaking to an ex-husband:

I would like you to send me the schedule for Matt's hockey games. I feel annoyed when you wait until the night before a game and then expect me to change my plans immediately.

Speaking to an ex-wife:

I feel concerned when you say how much you hate me in front of our daughter. Please address me privately if you're feeling angry with me.

WHEN THE "I" STATEMENT MEETS RESISTANCE

While "I" statements are helpful and powerful, they don't always engender the response that you'd like. "I" statements and positive assertions sometimes meet resistance because they go against a long-standing chain of command that was consciously or subconsciously set up in a marriage. Even though the marriage is over, it can be very frightening and difficult to change this dynamic. So even if you give the most well-formulated, concise, non-threatening "I" statement that ever came out of anyone's mouth, your ex may have a surprising or even shocking response.

For example, sometimes you'll give an "I" statement and come up against a brick wall. Your ex doesn't rant and rave; it just seems as though he or she doesn't "get it." In this case, you might want to try rephrasing your "I" statement to include a metaphor. Metaphors are stories that paint a picture similar to the one at hand. They have a way of depersonalizing an issue and presenting it in a clear, non-threatening manner that can penetrate even the thickest skin.

For example, say your ex fails to change his behavior when you say, "I feel ignored when you keep looking at your phone. Please give me your undivided attention." Rephrase your thought in an arena that is familiar to the person to whom you're talking. If your ex enjoys basketball, then liken your comment to the game.

When we discuss Tommy's failing grades and you keep looking at your phone, I feel as if I'm the coach of a basketball team and one of my players keeps shooting baskets while I talk. How is that player going to contribute to the team effort when he won't give his attention to the team meeting? I would really appreciate it if you would give me your full attention while we're talking.

It's important to keep your metaphors short and to include what you want your ex to do differently. Remember that the metaphor is not a substitute for an "I" statement and positive assertion; it's a different presentation of it when your ex didn't get it the first time.

WHEN YOUR EX DOESN'T GIVE A $@#% HOW YOU FEEL

Other times, an ex may be so entrenched in his old style of responding that he'll rant and rave no matter what you say. If your ex responds to your new communication skill with, "I don't give a $@#% how you feel," then knowing what you want ahead of time and using a non-threatening, non-defensive statement will help combat this. For example, you might say, "I understand that. I can hear it in your voice." Then repeat what you want. "I'd like you to . . ."

If your ex continues to be abusive, disengage immediately to give both of you some time to cool off. Say, "I hear how angry you are. Let's take a break and come back to this another time."

SAVE THE SARCASM

Some people consider sarcasm witty and fun, and it can be when used correctly. But in a delicate discussion with your ex it is fuel for a fire, especially if you're pointing out a negative trait. Again, using the analogy of a business relationship, if your client said, "Let's meet on Tuesday at nine," would you ever respond with, "Oh, sure, especially since you're always bright and cheery at that hour"?

Sarcasm, both as a verbal statement and in its non-verbal form, eye rolling, is a form of contempt, which is a hostile behavior and has no place in your parenting relationship.

DISENGAGING

To disengage during a conversation with your ex, it's helpful to plan ahead with a scripted excuse that frees you if the communication becomes hostile. Planning ahead ensures that you're less likely to become rattled when old patterns and negative cycles rear their ugly heads. You can even present the limits of your conversation at the beginning and say, "I have a few other commitments today, so this will have to be brief."

If your ex becomes verbally abusive, you can say, "We'll have to continue this another time, because I have to . . ." and give the excuse that you planned ahead of time. This ensures that your emotions don't get the best of you and helps you present yourself as efficient, calm, and collected, even if you're shaking in your boots!

Here are a few suggestions:

I have to go. Someone's at the door. I'll speak with you later.

I have to go. I have an appointment with my accountant [doctor, hairdresser, dentist].

I have to go. I'm meeting a friend. We'll talk another time.

I have to go. I promised a friend that I'd pick up her child.

I have to go. I have to get a letter in the mail.

I need to pick up the dry cleaning before they close. We'll have to finish in a few minutes.

Once you give your excuse to disengage, pull out your appointment book and schedule another time to talk. By scheduling another time right away, your ex won't assume you're avoiding him or her and you will remain in the position of power. In other words, it won't look as though you're turning tail and running, even if you are.

Disengaging during a conversation with your ex will give you the opportunity to collect yourself and set yourself up for success if a boundary isn't being respected.

SETTING YOURSELF UP FOR SUCCESS

When you top the problem pyramid, it's generally because there is a boundary you'd like respected or a rule you'd like followed and your ex isn't complying in some way. Basically, the "I" statement and positive assertion inform your ex about these new rules in a clear, direct way. But when this doesn't work, we don't want you to stand there feeling helpless. There are still actions you can take that will empower you and get the point across to your ex that you're serious about your boundaries.

We communicate the seriousness of our words when we're willing to follow through with actions. In order to be effective, any action you decide to take needs to be firm and impersonal, not punitive or disrespectful. It should be directly linked to the problem and respectfully communicated. The idea is not for you to get revenge on your ex but to come up with something that will work for you as well as encourage your ex to acknowledge and respect the boundary next time. For example, if you have a hairdresser's appointment at ten and your ex misses the nine thirty pickup and shows up at ten fifteen, he might find a note on your door explaining that you had an appointment, with directions to where he can pick up your child.

TAGGING POSITIVE ASSERTIONS WITH A CHOICE

The most effective limit setting includes a choice. Giving your ex a choice ahead of time helps her not feel blindsided at the last moment, which is likely to trigger feelings of anger and revenge. If you know that your ex is always late, for example, you can tag your positive assertion with the action you will take if she doesn't adhere to the limit. For example:

> *I feel frustrated when you arrive late. Please pick up Justin by nine or I'll take him to your sister's house and you can pick him up there.*

Tagging a positive assertion with a choice simply involves adding the word "or" to the assertion and telling your ex what action you will take if your request isn't honored.

Choices focus the listener on his options in a particular situation. Because there is a choice, your ex will feel as though he has some control over the situation. When a person feels as though he has control, he's less likely to resist or break the limit. On the other hand, if you were to threaten him with,

"You'd better get here on time, or I'm going to take our daughter to your sister's house and you can just pick her up there," it's not likely that your ex will arrive on time in the future.

MEANING WHAT YOU SAY

When you offer a choice to your ex, it's important to be sure that you're comfortable with it. If your ex's sister won't be home, for example, or you're concerned that your daughter will be upset about being dropped off there, you don't want to offer this as a choice. Otherwise, you'll be caught in the position of not being able to follow through with what you said. The next time that your ex is late, he'll know that your choices are really empty threats and he won't take you seriously. This weakens your position and makes your ex more resistant to other limits you're trying to enforce.

BRAINSTORMING SOLUTIONS TO YOUR PROBLEMS

Many people feel that coming up with creative choices or actions is the most difficult part of this technique, but in reality, everybody has the capability to problem-solve creatively. Like other things, this skill grows easier with practice.

A helpful technique to set the gears of creativity in motion and increase your repertoire of useful actions is to brainstorm about what choices are viable. To do this, start with the assumption that no idea is stupid. The goal of brainstorming is to throw every solution you can think of on the proverbial table, including the unrealistic and outrageous ones. Sometimes "crazy" ideas lead to the solution that works.

You can brainstorm in any shape and form, but for now use a paper and colorful pen, preferably a felt-tip or one with ink that flows freely. Write your problem in its simplest form across the top. Then write anything that comes to mind. Write across the paper; write down the sides; doodle. Take a break for a few minutes. During this time relax, breathe, stretch, turn on the radio and listen to the words of a song you like, and try to clear your mind. Then go back and weed out some of the more unrealistic or unfeasible ideas. It can take minutes or days to come up with creative solutions. It takes as much time as it takes. If you have a creative friend, ask him or her to help with your process.

Take a look at a few of the actions that we brainstormed for a consistently late ex and see what other choices you might be able to offer. For example, if you have a tween or teen, you could leave and ask your child to lock up when her mother picks her up. Or you could take your child with you so that when your ex arrives he finds a note explaining where you went and the time you'll be back so he can pick up your child then. You could also find a babysitter who'll come over on the spur of the moment and charge the babysitter's fee to your ex. Or maybe you could run off to Hawaii and ignore the problem!

This process can go on and on. The point is to shift gears from the "poor me, what am I going to do?" to the "I wonder if this would work?" attitude. Many of the solutions you come up with may be unfeasible, like running off to Hawaii (though you'd probably really like to!). But once you give yourself permission to brainstorm all the possibilities, you can then choose your best ideas and tag them onto a positive assertion. Let's see how that might sound:

Please arrive on time, or our daughter can lock things up when the two of you leave.

Please arrive on time, or I'll have to leave for my appointment and you can pick our son up later.

Please arrive on time, or I'll have the babysitter watch our daughter until you get here and you can pay the sitter when you pick our daughter up.

Please arrive on time, or you can pick up our daughter at your sister's house.

Please arrive on time, or I'm running off to Hawaii and charging the trip to you!

AVOIDING ALL-OR-NOTHING TRAPS

Sometimes we get stuck in the brainstorming process because we have trouble seeing shades of gray. Very often we'll see a situation as all or nothing, black or white, when there are actually many different choices available. For example, if you're crossing the street and the sign says: "Don't walk," you may think that you don't have a choice. You have to stand where you are until the light changes. But, in truth, you could cross the street against the light (and chance getting hit by a car). This choice is so obvious, however, that we often don't think of it as a choice at all.

Another possibility would be to walk down the street to another corner (which may take you out of your way) and cross when the light changes there. Or you could just go home and forget about crossing the street. Remember that even if you don't like some of the choices or if they're not feasible to implement, those choices still exist.

TAKING IT SLOWLY

Sometimes, no matter how good your "I" statement is and no matter how well and equitably you phrased your positive assertion and choice, you will still meet with resistance. When this happens, remember to imagine yourself back in that business meeting. When a good businessperson is faced with a resistant client, one of the first things that comes to mind is, *This is going to take some time. I'll need to take it slowly. She isn't sold on this yet and I don't want to blow it; there's a lot of money involved.* Conversely, when you are faced with a resistant ex-spouse, your first thought is usually, *Here we go again. If I don't get my point across now, I'll never get it across. There's a lot at stake here, and I'm going to make her see that!* Recognize the difference?

When faced with resistance, it's important to take things slowly. It takes time to develop your relationship with your ex into a working relationship, especially since the relationship didn't work while you were married.

ASKING QUESTIONS

When your ex is resisting the limit or solution you're proposing, try asking non-threatening questions. Asking questions makes your ex feel as though you're interested in what he or she has to say. It also gives you a wealth of information that you didn't have previously but can now draw on. An ex who is involved in creating the solution is less likely to object to it later on. For example:

Instead of: "I can't believe you don't see my side."
Ask: "What would you suggest I do in this situation?"

Instead of: "You'd better shape up or I"ll be forced to take action."
Ask: "Tell me more about what you're looking for."

Instead of: "We're going to do this my way or not at all."
Ask: "How do you see this working?"

Instead of: "I can't believe what a jerk you are."
Ask: "How do you think we could work this out?"

ROLE-PLAY: DOING YOUR HOMEWORK

If you have an ex who is exceedingly difficult or if you simply have an exceedingly difficult time with your ex, it might be helpful to practice the techniques you've learned on someone else. Preparation through role-play is often a good investment of your time because it helps you change old patterns of behavior in a neutral, friendly environment where you won't feel as though the mistakes you might make are a matter of life and death.

Enlist the aid of a good friend to play your ex so that you can practice your new skills before trying them in a real-life situation. To do this, project what your ex's objections might be and tell those objections to a friend. Have him or her be as mean and nasty as he or she can be during the exchange to give you the practice you need for the worst-case scenario. (More than likely, your friend will be tougher than your ex.) Open the conversation with your "I" statement. If you have a weak point, put it on the table first—it will lose its power that way. Remember to be businesslike, clear, and firm during the conversation. Then turn the tables and have your friend pretend to be you and you play your ex. Because your friend doesn't have the same history as you do with your ex, you're likely to glean some good ideas, not only by listening to the words he uses but also listening to his tone of voice and watching his body language.

SUMMING IT UP

"I" statements and positive assertions will play a big part in creating successful communication with your ex. Knowing in advance what you want and what your limits are, as well as what action you can take if your ex ignores your requests, will empower you and bring you closer to both your personal goals and a successful divorce.

5.

Problems That You Need to Solve

WORKING THROUGH THE PROBLEMS

Now that you know what techniques to use when you top the problem pyramid, let's work through some of the real-life problems we mentioned in chapter 1. We'll walk you through an interpretation of what's happening by identifying the problem and looking at the feelings and thoughts that are present. When it's appropriate, we'll also give you an example of one possible "I" statement and positive assertion plus whatever choice you might offer in that situation.

MY EX CAN DO NO WRONG

My son thinks his dad can do no wrong. But my ex lies to us all the time. He says he can't pick up our son on Saturday morning because he has to work. When I call his office to offer to drop Danny off, he's not there. It makes me crazy!

What is the problem here?

My ex lies to us, and Danny thinks his dad is God!

Is the problem that your ex lies or that your son thinks he's God?

Both!

Okay, let's take these issues separately. First, we'll look at the problem of your ex lying to you.

Who tops the problem pyramid when your ex lies?

Who has the upset feelings? You.

Who brought up the issue? You.

Who is responsible for implementing the solution? You.

What is your most intense feeling?

I feel crazy. And I'm frustrated.

What are the thoughts that are triggering your feelings of craziness and frustration?

I keep trying to get Danny and his dad to have quality time together. As I said, Danny adores his father. But his dad keeps getting out of the visitation by lying to me. Why should I waste my time and energy getting them together when his dad is such a jerk? That's why I feel so frustrated. And then when Danny thinks his father can do no wrong, right after dad just lied to me, I get crazy!

You asked a good question: Why should you waste your time and energy trying to get them together?

Well . . . I guess because I feel like Danny needs time with his dad.

Can you change the lying?

No.

Can you change how Danny's father feels about visitation and/ or Danny?

No.

Is this worth your time and energy trying to change what can't be changed?

I guess not.

Many parents agonize over the relationship (or lack thereof) between their ex and their children. In fact, many divorced parents say it's one of the biggest factors in their daily worrying and guilt. The problem, of course, is that we can't control relationships that belong to other people. So our advice here would be this:

Stop calling Danny's dad to try to find a way to get him and your son to see each other. Hear the message that your ex is sending you with his behavior—he doesn't want to see Danny this weekend, period. Accept that the relationship between Danny and his father is on a path of its own and that either it will work itself out or it won't.

As for Danny thinking his father can do no wrong, it *is* hard when you see your ex in one light and your child sees him in another. Keep in mind, though, that if your ex continues to behave inappropriately, your son will eventually see that for himself.

CHANGING PLANS

My ex is constantly changing her plans and then expects me to change mine. I'm really tired of it. But what can I do? If my ex cancels visitation at the last minute, I can't leave the kids alone.

What is the problem here?

My ex is inconveniencing me over and over so I can't make any plans.

Try this exercise: Whenever you use the word "can't," replace it with the word "won't." As we mentioned in a previous chapter, this simple switch will empower you to take responsibility for things that you can control.

My ex is inconveniencing me over and over, so I won't *make any plans.*

Now, what is the problem here?

I'm being inconvenienced by my ex and I'm not making plans because I hate having to rearrange them at the last minute.

So who tops the problem pyramid?

Who has the upset feelings? You.

Who brought up the issue? You.

Who is responsible for implementing the solution? You.

What is the most intense feeling?

I feel inconvenienced and frustrated.

What thoughts are causing those feelings?

I want to be able to make plans and know that they'll happen the way I planned. That rarely happens because of my ex's last-minute changes.

So is this worth investing your time and energy to change?

Yes. I'd like to make plans and be able to stick with them.

Now it's time to formulate an "I" statement with a positive assertion, remembering to make it gender sensitive:

I feel inconvenienced when plans are changed at the last minute. Please give me forty-eight hours' notice if you need to change your plans.

What if your ex-wife doesn't respond? What if she agrees to the forty-eight hours' notice but doesn't observe it? Then it's time to tag the positive assertion with a choice:

Please call me forty-eight hours in advance or I'll call a babysitter and you can pay.

Keep in mind that if you tell your ex you're charging the babysitter's fee to her, you must be sure to follow through. If she picks up your child late, have the sitter ask her for the money. If your ex doesn't show up at all, type up a bill and mail it. If it's not paid promptly, send a "past due" notice thirty days later.

The key here is not allowing yourself to be inconvenienced. In not making plans because your ex is unreliable, you essentially enable that very behavior in her. Your ex doesn't have to change because there's no reason to. On the other hand, if you go ahead and make your plans, including alternate arrangements for your child in case your ex doesn't come through, you not only get what you want, you also help your ex to understand the consequences of her actions.

IN YOUR FACE ON FACEBOOK

My ex is big on Facebook and Twitter, and he's all over it with the kids and what they do each weekend, posting photos or reporting: "Here we are at the park" or "Here we are at the zoo." I miss my kids terribly on weekends and find that this just makes me miss them more. How can I get him to leave the kids out of his Facebook life?

What is the problem here?

I miss my kids on weekends and seeing them with my ex on Facebook makes me feel terrible.

When you use the word "terrible" what do you mean?

I guess I mean I feel jealous that he gets to be with them and I don't.

Who tops the problem pyramid?

Who has the upset feelings? You.

Who brought up the issue? You.

Who is responsible for implementing the solution? You.

What is the most intense feeling?

Jealousy, I guess. But I guess I also feel lonely when they're not around.

What thoughts are causing those feelings?

Well, I think to myself, how come he gets to do the "fun" stuff with them while I have to do the "drudge" work during the week, like supervising homework and getting them to and from school? And then all the fun they have is posted all over Facebook like he's the big hero or something.

Anything else? About the loneliness?

I don't know. I guess I wonder sometimes if I'll ever have fun again. I seem to spend my weekends just catching up on chores and moping around the house because the kids aren't here.

So what's the problem that needs your time and energy here? Is it about getting your ex to not post on Facebook? Or is it really about finding a cure for your loneliness and making sure you have times when you feel like you're having fun with your kids?

Yeah. I guess that's it. I need to find something to get me out of the house on weekends. And I need to plan fun things to do with the kids during the time I have them.

Sometimes, when we untangle a problem that we own, we discover that it's not about changing the other person's behavior but really about changing our own. This mom feels like many do—her ex gets all the glory while she's left with the daily grind. After a divorce, it becomes especially important that you do two things:

1. Schedule time to have fun with your kids. We're not talking about something expensive and time-consuming, like a weekend skiing (although that can be fun, too, and is an option if you can afford it). We're talking about simple things you can do in between their homework assignments (like watching a YouTube video together) or being creative about dinner plans (having a picnic on the floor). These small, relationship-building activities can help you feel more connected to your kids on a daily basis and break up the routine that often feels like work.

2. Create a life for yourself. When we get married and then have children, we find ourselves submerged in the persona of wife/husband and mother/father. When you discard your role of wife or husband, you need to rediscover who *you* are. Take up a hobby; sign up for the gym; start a book group; heck, develop a Facebook profile of your own (just don't use it against your ex!). Loneliness and jealousy are common after a divorce, and both are things about which you can take action.

BLOCKBUSTER BUST

The trailers for the new blockbuster movie looked great and I really wanted to take my son. I couldn't take him to the opening, though, because his dad had him then, so we agreed that we'd go the following weekend. But when he came home from his dad's, he told me they'd already seen it. I was told, "It was *great!*" I wanted to kill my ex!!! How dare he? My son knew that I was looking forward to seeing the movie with him and then his father pulls the rug out from under our plans. He does this all the time—he constantly undermines the fun things I have planned with our son.

What is the problem here?

My ex undermined my plans.

Who tops the problem pyramid?

Who has the upset feelings? You.

Who brought up the issue? You.

Who is responsible for implementing the solution? You.

What is the most intense feeling?

I feel undermined. And really, really disappointed because I was looking forward to seeing the movie with my son.

What thoughts are causing that feeling?

I wanted to go to the movie with my son. Why does my ex always have to one-up me?

There are two problems here. One is that you and your son didn't go to the movie like you planned. The other is that, as far as you can tell, your ex planned this as a way of undermining you, because it sounds like he's done that before.

Exactly.

So let's look first at your disappointment about not seeing the movie with your son. Is it possible that your son could have some responsibility here? Couldn't he have told his father that you and he had made plans to go to the movie together?

Well, I guess so. Yes.

So really, your first "I" statement and positive assertion should be to your son. (Note that in this case the parent will tag the "I" statement with a choice, which essentially becomes the positive assertion):

> *I feel really disappointed that we didn't get to see the movie together like we planned. Next time I'd like you to either consult with me first if you're changing our plans or make a different plan with your dad.*

It's easy to blame your ex for all the things that go wrong, especially if you feel disappointed, jealous, and undermined. The truth is, though, that no matter how awful your ex is, there is often shared responsibility for the problems that arise. When you express your disappointment to your child about his part in a decision, you help him begin to think for himself and take responsibility for his actions. This is an important part of growing up. The goal is not, however, to make your child feel guilty; it's simply to make him aware of your feelings as well as of his responsibility to stick with a commitment, even if that commitment is made lightly. To that end, it's very important that you keep your tone of voice and body language matter-of-fact and respectful.

Now, what about this parent's feeling of being undermined by her ex? Let's ask this: Is it possible that your ex didn't actually know you were going to take your son to this particular movie?

Well, it's possible, I guess. But he does have a pattern of doing this regardless.

So, two things: First, avoid assumptions. While there may indeed be a pattern of behavior on the part of your ex, if you automatically assume that he undermined you, you may be starting a fire rather than putting one out. Don't blame without the facts. Second, if he did know and did deliberately undermine you, then there are two things you should do:

1. Use an "I" statement and positive assertion:

The next time you take our son to a new movie, I'd like you to check with me first to make sure he and I don't already have plans to see it together. I feel disappointed that he and I didn't get to go like we'd talked about.

2. Recognize the pattern.

The preceding "I" statement and positive assertion is excellent in that it's gender appropriate, calm, and respectful. That being said, if your ex has a history of undermining you, it's not likely to have an effect. Here's where it's helpful to recognize your ex's patterns of behavior. If he has a history of doing things like this, then you can avoid disappointment on your part by knowing ahead of time that this might happen. If the "big blockbuster" is on his weekend, it's likely that he'll choose to take your son, so plan something for a weekend when you do have your child with you or ask your ex to switch weekends.

PARTY TIME

When the kids go to visit their father for the weekend, it's party time. He feeds them junk, lets them stay up all night to watch R-rated movies, and has no regard for their personal hygiene. Late Sunday night, he returns them feeling sick, tired, and dirty. I have a terrible time getting them up for school on Monday.

What is the problem here?

Well, I really object to their father's values. I mean, can you imagine? He lets them watch these violent movies! And then they eat all this junk. And who suffers? Me, on Monday morning, when they're cranky and feeling sick.

There are actually several problems here: Your values are different from your ex's. You object to your children watching R-rated movies. They eat junk food when they're there. You're suffering because you have to deal with them when they finally arrive home.

So who tops the problem pyramid?

Who has the upset feelings? You.

Who brought up the issue? You.

Who is responsible for implementing the solution? You.

What is the most intense feeling?

I feel angry.

What thoughts are causing that feeling?

I have to suffer on Monday mornings because my ex lets our kids stay up too late and eat junk.

Is it worth your time and energy to change?

Absolutely, I can't take it anymore!

What, specifically, is causing you to suffer on Monday mornings? That your ex doesn't bathe your children? That he lets them stay up too late over the weekend? That he allows them to eat junk? That he allows them to watch violent movies?

> *Well, I'm mad about all of it, but I guess the thing that affects Monday mornings is that they're exhausted and cranky from the weekend.*

When asked to look more closely at the problem, this mother decided that the primary issue was her children's exhaustion on Monday mornings. While she didn't like the other values that her ex was espousing and living by over the weekend, she quite rightly realized that none of them presented an imminent danger to her children. In addition, controlling what happens at her ex's house is an unrealistic goal, and should she adopt it, she would set herself up to fail.

So what's your "I" statement/positive assertion with regard to Monday mornings?

I want you to return the children early on Sunday, bathed and well rested.

It's interesting to note that in this case the positive assertion is all that's needed. Feelings might just complicate the matter, so there's no need to include them. But now that you've formulated the positive assertion, look at it closely. Of course you'd like to have the children bathed, but does it really affect Monday morning for you?

Well, no, I guess not.

So reformulate your positive assertion.

I want you to return the children early on Sunday and make sure they're well rested because it will make it easier for them to get up for school the next morning.

This is better. One nice thing about using this format is that it makes the communication very logical and concise. In addition, notice that this mother intuitively included a "because" statement that had to do with her children rather than with her.

Studies have shown that when people are asked to do something, they respond more readily if they're told the reason why. This works in divorce communication as well, but only if you make the "because" about something or someone other than you. By focusing on her children here she encourages her ex to see how his behavior impacts them on Monday mornings.

Mom also realized that it didn't make much sense to include all of her gripes (that they were dirty, that they eat junk food, that they watch violent movies) in her communication at this point. If she had, it likely would have overwhelmed her ex and caused him to respond as if he was being attacked. Always remember your primary goal: to evoke a change in behavior so that your situation gets better. It's *not* to do battle.

But what if her ex doesn't respond? Then she might tag the positive assertion with this choice:

> *Please return the children early and well rested on Sunday night, or go ahead and keep them until Monday morning and take them to school.*

Now, what about the other problems that the woman was having? What about the differing values, the R-rated movies, the junk food? Well, she could give an "I" statement and positive assertion about any of these. It's often easier, however, to begin with a problem from which you are directly suffering, as she did. In addition, as we mentioned previously, it's unlikely that her ex will change his values or stop the movies and junk food. If she wants to address these in the most effective way, it would be easier to point out to her children the natural consequences that these things have on them—they wind up feeling cranky and ill and may have the inconvenience of bathing on Monday morning rather than sleeping an extra ten minutes.

Note: While this book is more about problem solving than actual advice, many divorced parents have found that having the child go to a "neutral" place, like school, instead of right from Mom's to Dad's place or vice versa, is easier on the child. That way, the child doesn't have to deal with the conflicting feelings of saying good-bye to one parent and hello to the other at the same time. So this last assertion and choice, having Dad keep the kids until Monday morning and take them to school, might be the best for everyone involved. Other neutral alternatives are after-school activities, a friend's house, a birthday party, and so on.

VISITATION VIA SKYPE

My ex begged for more visitation time with the kids. Now that he got what he wanted, he doesn't actually take them more often—He thinks that talking to them on Skype counts as a visit! So I still have the child-care duties and he feels like he's fulfilled his paternal duties by video chatting.

What is the problem here?

My ex calls Skyping visitation and it still leaves me with the child-care duties.

Is the problem about the Skyping or that you're left with the child-care duties?

Well, hmmm . . . I guess the Skyping is okay. I mean, they do get to see and talk to him every day because of it and before Skype they only saw him on his day of the week and alternate week-ends. But I resent that I have no time to myself, because if he actually took them, I'd have a free weekend from time to time.

So it sounds like Skype is actually beneficial to your ex's relationship with the kids—which is positive. Maybe the real issue is that you don't have enough free time—regardless of Skype.

Yeah. I think that's true.

So who tops the problem pyramid?

Who has the upset feelings? You.

Who brought up the issue? You.

Who is responsible for implementing the solution? You.

What's your feeling?

I feel overwhelmed because I don't have enough time to myself.

So is this worth investing your time and energy to change?

Yes. I really need a break from time to time.

We can see that when we sort through this situation it becomes clear that Skype isn't actually the problem. In fact, Skype is beneficial to the relationship these children have with their father. If, however, Mom had confronted her ex before thinking this through and focused on the technology rather than the real problem of not having enough time for herself, she might actually have done more damage than good.

As for needing a break, this is a very real and very common problem in most divorces, especially when custody is not divided exactly evenly. The question becomes: If she gives an "I" statement and positive assertion to her ex, will it change things? The answer is that it depends upon the level of empathy her ex has with regard to her needs. Let's look at how she might formulate that communication.

I'd like for you to take the kids to your house on the weekends that you have them. I feel overwhelmed when I have them all the time and I need a break.

Now this might work, and it's well worth trying. As the divorce relationship matures, it often becomes more convivial, which is why, even if this type of statement hasn't worked in the past, it's worth not giving up on.

Let's say that in this case it doesn't work. A possible choice to tag it with is:

Please take the children this weekend, or give me money for a babysitter.

Because this might be met with stony-cold silence, it's worthwhile (for your own sanity) to address the issue as if your ex weren't around at all. In other words, how can you use the resources you have to get that much-needed time for yourself? If you have financial resources, you could hire a babysitter. If you have community resources, you might ask a friend or neighbor to watch the kids. If you have family resources, you might ask your sister or brother to take the kids for the weekend. The point is that when you have a problem and your ex is uncooperative, it may not be worthwhile to invest your time and energy trying to get him to cooperate in solving that problem. Sometimes, utilizing your external resources is the fastest, most effective way to resolve things.

YOU'VE GOT MAIL!

When we were married, my husband and I vowed to never look at each other's email. Well, now that he's broken all those other vows, I don't think I need to honor this one completely. I changed my password the day he left, but he's never bothered to change his. And while I don't open his emails, I sometimes log into his account to see if he's read the ones I've sent him. And I read the subject lines. So now I've figured out that he's dating someone and I think he's looking to buy a house. But when I ask him if he's dating someone and thinking of moving, he denies it!

What is the problem here?

My husband is lying to me about dating and moving.

Do those lies affect his relationship or visitation with your children? Do they affect your schedule or inconvenience you in any way?

Well, no, but it bugs me. And I'd like to know if he's dating so I can handle it with my children.

While we could say that this parent tops the problem pyramid because she has upset feelings and is raising the issue, the truth is that we would be evading the bottom line here. After a divorce you need *more* boundaries, not fewer. Invading your ex's privacy is inappropriate and will create problems that might never have come up otherwise. Even though this mother would like to be able to appropriately address her ex's dating if her children have feelings about it, she's borrowing trouble by spying on him. When he's ready to tell both her and the children that he's dating, then she can emotionally support her children through the process. Meanwhile, she should take whatever measures necessary so she's not tempted to spy.

A RECAP

As you read through the following recap, remember that the steps we're asking you to follow have the ultimate purpose of helping you interpret what's going on when a problem arises. Sometimes you'll need to work through the steps in the exact order in which they appear. Other times you might skip a step or find that one step leads you to a particular insight that redirects all the steps that follow.

The purpose of giving you these tools is to allow you to become more flexible, gain insight into your problems, and ultimately come up with a solution that leads to more happiness for you and your children. If you find yourself becoming rigid about following the steps exactly, take a break and come back to the problem at another time. Rigidity is not compatible with problem solving, and an inflexible attitude will only ensure that you spend time and energy on something that probably won't lead to a solution.

1. Decide what the problem is in its simplest form. Include only what is directly affecting you.
2. Determine who tops the problem pyramid.
3. Examine your Think-Feel-Do cycle and name the most intense feeling you have.
4. Recognize the thoughts that are causing your feelings.
5. Ask if it's worth your time and energy to change this situation or solve this problem.
6. If yes, formulate an "I" statement and positive assertion. Decide to whom you should address these: ex or child.
7. Tag the assertion with a choice if necessary.
8. Remember to give choices that you can follow through on.

6.

Learning to Cooperate with Your Ex

WORKING AT CHANGE

Cooperation means working together toward a common goal. Fostering a spirit of cooperation with your ex means laying down your weapons in the war of divorce in order to protect your children. It means that when your ex begins to argue with you, you don't argue back. It means that you stop being reactive and start being proactive. Your children should be your priority, and although it may kill you to share them with a jerk, it will hurt them irreparably if you and your ex continue to do battle.

It's understandable that you may feel bitter, angry, and vengeful toward your ex, but when you deliberately badmouth or argue with him or her in front of the children it's as if you're saying each harsh word to your kids themselves. The hurt and confusion they feel at those times is damaging. We know that nobody's perfect. And obviously there will be times when your child overhears you arguing with your ex, sees the expression on your face, or senses your underlying (and many times valid) disgust and anger. You're human. The point is that no matter what your feelings are, your children will be better off if you make them your central focus and work diligently at keeping the parenting relationship civil and cooperative.

There are two ways to work at change with your ex. One is by changing your internal state. First, you sort through your angry and bitter feelings. Your insights into those feelings enable you eventually to change them. Once your feelings are different, your actions automatically change. This is often a lengthy process and many times requires the professional assistance of a counselor.

Another way to change is by changing your actions first, no matter how you feel. It's akin to administering CPR to someone whose heart has stopped. You can't get inside the person and restart the heart by changing the internal state, so instead, you work from the outside. You place your hands over the person's breastbone and push down at regular intervals. This external force eventually changes the internal state, and the heart begins beating.

By learning the cooperation skills presented in this chapter, you're essentially administering CPR to the parenting relationship. When you change your actions in an argument with your ex, eventually your internal state will change, too. Remember that although it's okay to allow the marital relationship to die, it's not okay for the parenting relationship to die, because if it does, it's your children who will suffer.

THE FIGHT-OR-FLIGHT RESPONSE

When you find yourself in a stressful situation, your subconscious automatically assesses your physiological response (sweaty palms, fast heartbeat, rapid breathing, shaking hands, cracking voice) in order to determine what kind of signal it should send to your body. Should it tell your body to run from danger? Should it tell your body to prepare defenses and fight? Or should it tell your body that everything's fine, that you should sit down, relax, and have a cup of tea?

The problem with what your subconscious finds is that it's not discriminatory. It can't tell the difference between the rapid breathing that occurs because you are furious that your ex won't take your child to a birthday party and the rapid breathing that happens when you realize you're being pursued by a wild beast. In either case, your subconscious sends the same message: Run, fight, or be eaten! This panic signal effectively shuts down the part of your brain that handles language and rational thought. Your reactions include clenched fists, gritted teeth, red face, slamming down the phone, crying, and probably a few others. In other words, you respond on a purely physiological level. When that happens, you become unresourceful and ineffective and you give away your power and control over the situation.

Altering the Fight-or-Flight Response

Speaking to an ex often evokes a fight-or-flight response. One father we watched would get red in the face and clench the arms of the chair until his knuckles turned white. He stuttered at the mere suggestion that he talk about what he would say to his ex. Invariably, the first words out of his mouth were explosive at best and profane at worst. Beginning a discussion with profanity and name-calling (even if that's the way you feel) is not cooperative. When your blood pressure has already risen or your hands are shaking, you considerably weaken your position. We wouldn't presume to suggest that you can rid yourself of anxiety or rage completely, but you can use techniques that will calm, center, and focus you enough to enable you to stay powerful and in control during an argument.

DEEP BREATHING: A TECHNIQUE THAT CALMS

Breathing deeply breaks into the cycle between your subconscious and your body and gives you an alternative to the fight-or-flight response. When you breathe deeply, you alter the message that your subconscious receives. In essence, you send the message to your subconscious that there is nothing to be afraid of. After all, if there were, you certainly wouldn't be standing around taking time to breathe! When you change the message you send to your brain, it stops sending the panic signals that make you ineffective and less resourceful.

To be an effective deep breather, you must practice. Begin by practicing in front of the mirror. Don't rush. Breathe in deeply enough to fill your lungs, then sit or stand straighter and take in just a little extra. Breathe out slowly. Count as you inhale and then as you exhale. Say, "That's one." Breathe again. Say, "That's two." One more time: "That's three." This technique is useful not only during a conversation with your ex when you find yourself reacting but also prior to phoning or meeting your ex. And if three breaths don't seem to be altering the fight-or-flight response, take more.

Don't Hurry!

When you believe that you must respond immediately to whatever your ex says and you rush to fill in the silences in a conversation, you inevitably engage the fight-or-flight reaction. In addition, you place yourself at a disadvantage by not allowing yourself time to think. It's not only okay to allow silence (and breathing) in a conversation; it's necessary.

If your ex is continuing to talk or shouting at you to answer him or her, take the phone away from your ear for a moment. If you're face-to-face, close your eyes. It's difficult to count breaths when you're staring at someone you don't like very much. Closing your eyes momentarily shuts down your visual sense. If you find it difficult to breathe deeply and incur silence, then practice during your conversations with friends and family members. It may feel awkward at first, but soon you'll discover that the pressure to speak disappears. And remember not to cover your silences with "um." Silence is much more powerful.

SHIFTING YOUR MIND-SET

Part of the difficulty in cooperating with your ex may lie in your tendency to rehearse negative thoughts about him. Much like the self-defeating self-talk we discussed earlier, these thoughts engage and propel you into a negative Think-Feel-Do cycle. For example, you think, *I hate him; I hate him; I wish he would die.* If you repeatedly think this while listening to him describe why he doesn't have time to take your child shopping for camp, it sets you up to fail because you will plan your next action based on these negative thoughts. Likewise, the self-defeating self-talk you engage in prior to a conversation with your ex sets you up to fail. You may have thoughts like: *I can't do this, she's just going to start screaming at me again* or *Why do I even bother talking to her? She's such a jerk.* This rehearsal of negative, angry thoughts serves only to make you more angry and negative. It robs you of momentum and power and creates a tendency for you to respond argumentatively instead of cooperatively.

Alternative Thoughts

Rather than rehearsing your anger, frustration, or anxiety when you need to discuss something with your ex, write down some alternative thoughts prior to the discussion. Memorize them, like an actor memorizes lines. As artificial or awkward as it may seem at first, you'll find that you can create a more powerful position for yourself by rehearsing positive thoughts prior to speaking to your ex. The key is in the rehearsal. You don't even have to believe these thoughts. If you rehearse and use them, you'll find they can change your entire composure during a conversation.

To demonstrate, we've listed some common negative thoughts that people have about their exes and a more positive (and thus more powerful) thought to replace them:

Negative Thought: *I hate him.*
Positive Thought: *I can handle my anger*

Negative Thought: *What's her problem?*
Positive Thought: *I'm just going to listen.*

Negative Thought: *He's such a slime bag!*
Positive Thought: *I'm capable of dealing with all kinds of people.*

Negative Thought: *I can't stand the sound of her voice.*
Positive Thought: *I can listen to the content of the conversation and ignore her tone of voice.*

Negative Thought: *He makes me sick!*
Positive Thought: *I can handle my uncomfortable feelings.*

Negative Thought: *I wish I could rip her tongue out.*
Positive Thought: *I am above physical violence.*

Negative Thought: *He always puts me down.*

Positive Thought: *It doesn't matter what he thinks of me; we're no longer married.*

GETTING WHAT WE GIVE

Dr. Henry Grayson, in his book *Mindful Loving: 10 Practices for Creating Deeper Connections,* tells of a fascinating experiment he once performed with his wife. While he was at work all day on alternating days of a two-week period, he thought only loving thoughts about his wife, recalling their best times together and all her good qualities. On the other days, he dismissed the good thoughts and recalled only judgmental, critical, and resentful thoughts about her. On the positive-thought days, when he got home his wife would meet him at the door with a kiss and they'd have a great evening. On the negative days, it was almost uncanny that she'd be somewhere else in the apartment when he came home. Then she'd appear a few minutes later, grumpy, and they'd have some sort of spat that night. This led him to conclude that others can "sense" our thoughts much more than we realize and that we "get back what we give out" in life.

Practicing positive thoughts about your ex will set the stage for cooperation between the two of you.

LISTENING TO UNDERSTAND

The basis for cooperation lies in being able to communicate effectively, and the foundation for good communication lies in the ability to listen. Stephen R. Covey, in his best-selling book, *The 7 Habits of Highly Effective People: Powerful Lessons in Personal Change,* writes that if he had to choose the single most important thing he's learned in the field of interpersonal relations, it would be this: "Seek first to understand, then to be understood." Listening to and trying to understand your ex is far more powerful than you might realize.

That being said, listening is a skill. While we do it quite naturally with the people whom we feel close to, it doesn't come nearly so easily when we feel accepted, misheard, or wronged. Learning the skill of listening, rather than relying upon an innate understanding of it, is beneficial.

Listening can be broken down into four components: attention, acknowledgment, reflection, and restatement.

The First Component of Listening: Attention

Listening is more than just waiting your turn to speak, more than just being quiet, and more than just hearing the other person's words. The other person needs to feel as though he or she is being understood and treated respectively. We help him or her feel heard when we give him or her our full attention—a critical part of the listening process. This means looking your ex in the eyes, keeping your arms and legs uncrossed, and fully facing him or her. When your body language communicates an attitude of attention, the other person softens his or her attack because he or she no longer feels the need to work so hard to get his or her point across.

The Second Component of Listening: Acknowledgment

Acknowledgment means verbally or physically indicating that you're listening to the other person. Saying, "I see," "Uh-huh," and "Mmmm" are examples of how to verbally acknowledge that you're listening. Nodding, tilting your head and furrowing your brow inquisitively to use body language to accomplish the same goal.

It's important to understand that when you acknowledge that a problem exists or that your ex has a point, it doesn't mean that you are agreeing with him or her. For example, Andrew's ex-wife, Maggie, called him and began to complain about money. She said that she had taken an extra part-time job on Saturdays but was having trouble coming up with money to pay a babysitter during that time. Andrew got the feeling that she was taking a roundabout way to ask him for more financial support, which he was unwilling to give. Rather than reacting to his thoughts, however, he simply acknowledged her by saying, "Uh-huh . . . I see . . . I understand that you don't have the extra money for a babysitter on Saturdays. It's been a bad year for many of us, and eight hours adds up to a lot." Had Andrew reacted to his suspicions by exploding and saying, "I'm not giving you more money. How many times do I have to tell you that before you get it through your thick skull?" it would have provoked an argument, at the center of which would have been their child.

The Third Component of Listening: Reflection

Reflection goes hand in hand with acknowledgment. It requires that you try to determine what the other person might be feeling. This isn't easy. As you've already discovered, many times angry words or actions mask our more subtle emotions. "Reflection" refers not only to the process of looking underneath the masking emotion for the other person's more subtle feelings but also to being able to reflect those feelings back to him. This sounds something like, "I hear that you're feeling defensive about being late," or, "Sounds like you feel accused." When Andrew refused to engage with his ex, regarding her financial difficulties, she began to utilize some of the old dynamics that hadn't worked in the past. "Andrew, I don't know what I'm going to do. I can't afford a sitter; I just can't." Andrew responded with, "You really sound overwhelmed. Juggling work with a child is difficult."

The Fourth Component of Listening: Restatement

Many times people think they're clearly hearing someone when in fact they are interpreting what's being said. When Andrew listened to his wife complain about babysitting, he was sure that she was going to ask him for more money. Rather than explode at her with, "I'm not giving you more money," or, "What do you want from me anyway?" he restated what he thought she was saying: "Maggie, I think what I'm hearing you say is that you'd like me to cover the child-care expenses for you on Saturdays. Am I right?" To his surprise, she seemed bewildered: "Andrew, I'm not asking you for more money! I was just going to see if we could switch visitation from Wednesday nights to Saturdays so that time is covered for me for the next couple of months."

Beginning the restatement with, "I think what I'm hearing you say is . . . ," rather than with the more definitive, "I'm hearing you say . . . ," will keep your ex from feeling accused by you. Similarly, asking, "Am I right?" at the end of a restatement enables you to check in with the other person to see if you heard correctly. And it affords your ex the opportunity to correct you if you didn't.

FINDING AGREEMENT

Another important cooperation skill involves listening carefully to see if there are any points on which you can agree during an argument. Thinking back to our business relationship analogy, when a client is extremely resistant good businesspeople listen carefully to see if there are any points that they can agree on. The businesspeople think to themselves, *Could I agree, either in principle or in part, with any of what he* [or *she*] *is saying?* When they find even a part of a statement they can agree on, they seize that opportunity. It's akin to trying to turn an out-of-control horse around. Sometimes you have to ride the horse in the direction it's going before you can get it to respond to your words and actions.

When you're feeling attacked by your ex, it may be difficult to think in terms of agreement. You're far more likely to enter a negotiation with your ex with thoughts such as *She's such an idiot* or *He's one hundred percent wrong, as usual!* Yet when you look for points on which you can agree, you put yourself in the position of control and relay to your ex that you're working toward a common goal and resolution.

PULLING INSTEAD OF PUSHING

To better understand how agreement can work in your favor, try this exercise with another person. Face each other and clasp right hands. Both of you push as hard as you can. Feel the way your hands sway back and forth. See how little control there is. Now try it with your partner pushing while you pull toward you. Feel the difference? The same technique applies to verbal fighting. When you agree on some point, it's like pulling your opponent's hand toward you. You now have the control.

AVOIDING COMMUNICATION BLOCKS

Many times cooperative communication with an ex breaks down because we block it. Sometimes we deliberately do this and sometimes it's subconscious. It helps to recognize some common ways communication gets blocked: through interrupting, giving advice, invalidating another person's feelings or point of view, being defensive, critical, or contemptuous. Let's see how these sound.

Interrupting

Interrupting is one of the most common causes of communication breakdown. In an argumentative state, the thing people want most is to be heard. When you interrupt, you are not allowing the other person to finish his or her turn. You're not giving him or her a chance to feel "listened to." Remember that cooperation means working together. Let your ex finish what he or she has to say before you respond, and then request that your ex let you finish, as well.

Giving Advice

Another way to block the communication process is by offering unsolicited advice. When you become the adviser, the cooperative mood vanishes.

Sam was experiencing some sleep problems at home. His father, Steve, couldn't seem to get him to stay in bed at night until around eleven or twelve. Steve called his ex, Rachel, to see if she was experiencing the same difficulty on the nights Sam stayed with her.

"Rachel? It's Steve. I have a concern about Sam's sleeping habits and I wanted to ask you a question about it."

"What about it?"

"Well, I can't seem to get him to go to sleep until around midnight when he's here. I wondered if you were having a similar problem?"

"What you have to do," Rachel sighed, "is be firm. A little firmness goes a long way."

"I am being firm," Steve retorted.

"Well, clearly not firm enough. A boy needs a strong hand, especially from his father."

Steve's blood began to boil. "Are you accusing me of not being a good father? You are infuriating!" he yelled as he hung up the phone.

When Rachel responded to Steve's request for information by offering advice, she may have believed she was being helpful. After all, wasn't Steve asking for advice on getting their son to bed earlier in the evening? The problem is that we often give advice when we're simply being asked for information.

To keep communication with your ex cooperative, it's best to determine what your ex wants before dropping your pearls of wisdom. Steve and Rachel would have been better off had she employed her listening skills, then asked Steve if he wanted advice before giving it. She might have said something like, "It sounds like you're asking me what I would do, is that right?" He might then have responded with, "No, I just want to know if it's happening at your house as well."

Invalidating

Another effective communication block occurs when we invalidate another person's feelings or point of view. Everyone has and is entitled to his or her own opinions and feelings. By telling or even implying to another person that the opinions or feelings that he or she is experiencing are wrong, you invalidate legitimate concerns and are more likely to arouse anger than cooperation.

Josh's mother, Cheryl, called her ex because she was concerned about Josh using her ex's car during rush hour. She wanted to suggest that Josh be allowed to borrow the car only before five in the afternoon, when there wasn't much traffic, or after seven, when rush hour was over.

"Hank? It's Cheryl. Do you have a minute?"

"Sure."

"It's about Josh borrowing your car. I'm concerned about him driving in traffic—"

"Cheryl, you're being ridiculous!" Hank interrupted. "Josh is a good driver, and he'll be fine."

"Hank, I'm just trying to ask that you restrict his use of the car to non-rush hours."

"Look, Cheryl, there's nothing to be concerned about. Don't you have better things to do than worry?"

Not only did Hank interrupt Cheryl; he also invalidated what to her was a legitimate concern. Here is a major breakdown in what could have been a cooperative communication between Josh's parents.

Being Defensive

When you are most interested in defending yourself rather than listening, you block the communication and escalate the issue. Listen to how this sounds:

"Rachel? It's Steve. I have a concern about Sam's sleeping habits and I wanted to ask you a question about it."

"What about it?"

"Well, I can't seem to get him to go to sleep until around midnight when he's here. I wondered if you were having a similar problem?"

"Why would you think I have that problem? I'm a very good mother and I can handle him better than you can. It's not my fault that he doesn't listen to you."

Being Critical

Criticism is often conveyed when we use "you" statements. For example: "You forgot to pack Jamie's books again," "I can't believe you're late again," "You're being ridiculous." People often use criticism as a way of complaining about something. If you have a complaint, remember to use an "I" statement: "I feel frustrated when Jamie's books don't come back with him," "I'd like you to please be on time," "I feel overwhelmed." "I" statements don't place blame, which helps engage your ex in cooperation.

Having Contempt

Contempt is an attitude, usually conveyed by sarcasm, put-downs, teasing, or mocking. See how Hank's contempt for Cheryl gets communicated in the following conversation:

"It's about Josh borrowing your car. I'm concerned about him driving in traffic—"

"Cheryl, you're being ridiculous!" Hank interrupted. "Josh is a good driver, and he'll be fine."

"Hank, I'm just trying to ask that you restrict his use of the car to non-rush hours."

"Right, and we all know what a great driver you are. How many accidents have you had now? Three? Or is it four? I guess if he takes after you, we should buy him a helmet."

THE BOX STEP OF COOPERATIVE COMMUNICATION

Cooperative communication can be looked upon as a box step. Think of yourself as a partner in a dance. Imagine that you're drawing a box on the floor by moving your feet in that direction:

1. Step back—and assess the situation. You could, at this point, strike right back, but this action encourages retribution. Listen to understand, and remember that you don't have to make any decisions right this moment.
2. Step to the side—your ex's side. See if there is anything you can agree on. Look at what your ex's feelings, objectives, and motivation might be.
3. Step forward—present your ideas clearly and concisely. Remember to use "I" statements, not "you" statements.
4. Step to the other side—close your negotiation with a compromise.

Tim's mom was surprised when her ex called one day and began yelling. "You listen to me!" he said. "I am not going to have Tim riding a bike in the city. He's done fine up until now without a bike and I think it should stay that way."

Remembering the box step of cooperative communication, she refrained from engaging right away in an argument she knew nothing about. Instead, Sarah stepped back and went into a listening mode.

"I hear a lot of concern in your voice, George. What's going on?"

"Tim says you promised him a bike for his birthday, and I simply won't have it. It's far too dangerous to ride in the city."

Sarah then stepped to her ex's side, trying to hear it from his point of view and find something on which to agree. "I agree that it can be dangerous to ride on the streets."

She then stepped forward and presented her plan: "I had thought that I'd buy him a bike only if we limited his riding to the park, with a helmet to ensure his safety."

"Oh!" George seemed surprised, almost as if the wind had been knocked out of him. "I guess I didn't realize that."

Then Sarah stepped to the other side, closing the communication: "So can we agree that he can have a bike if he rides only in the park with a helmet?"

"Well, okay," George agreed, "and thanks."

When Sarah engaged George using her newly learned cooperation skills, she was able to calmly and effectively handle a situation that previously would have escalated into a fight.

CATCH 'EM DOING IT RIGHT

One of the most powerful ways to engage another person in cooperation is to acknowledge and appreciate his or her efforts.

Very often we watch for and pick on the things a person does wrong, incorrectly believing that if we point out his mistakes, it will help him change his behavior in the future. Unfortunately, this often makes the behavior worse—soon the person realizes that you'll never acknowledge what he did right anyway, so he or she might as well do it wrong. By watching for and acknowledging the things a person does right, however, you increase the likelihood that the person will do things right in the future. Even if you believe that your ex never does anything right, you'll find that this thougt process will move you in a more cooperative direction, even if you only acknowledge his efforts:

> *I know how hard it is for you to get out of the office on time. I appreciate that you made the effort today, even if it didn't work out.*

IF YOU LOSE IT COMPLETELY, APOLOGIZE

Working toward a cooperative relationship doesn't mean you'll achieve a perfect one. We're all human. Obviously, there will be times when you won't hold it together, when you'll lose your temper or composure in front of your ex. When this happens, apologize. It's not what you do but what you do afterward that counts. A simple "I'm sorry for calling you names" can go a long way. (This is an important point to remember when dealing with your kids, as well.)

GIVING YOURSELF PERMISSION TO COMPROMISE

Finally, cooperating with your ex for the sake of your child means compromise. Many people look at each conversation with their ex as a miniature battle to be won. If you look at it this way—hanging on to your thoughts of revenge, setting out to hurt your opponent, wanting to come out of every conversation the victor—you might end up winning each battle, but rest assured, you'll lose the war.

Your children are at stake here, and if their self-esteem suffers in your battles, which it most assuredly will, you will have lost much more than you ever realized. When you give yourself permission to compromise, you give yourself and your children permission to be happy. You've worked hard to get where you are today. Being a single parent is not an easy job. Raising a child is not easy. Cooperating with your ex reflects your maturity, sensitivity, and personal growth and, ultimately, makes things easier for you.

7.

When Your Child Tops the Problem Pyramid

PROTECTING YOUR CHILDREN

Prior to becoming a parent, you probably had no idea of the strength and fortitude you would need. From the round-the-clock feedings that exhausted you to your child's bumps and bruises that terrified you, each new experience stirred and continues to stir up deep feelings of responsibility. Most parents, when asked to describe the feelings they have about parenting, say that the guilt, joy, frustration, anger, and love are all overshadowed by the huge sense of being responsible for another person's life. And most parents concur that the intense amount of responsibility involved in taking care of a child can be overwhelming.

Because the responsibility is so huge, parents feel very protective of their children. Whether it involves an injured arm because he fell or hurt feelings because someone was rude or thoughtless to her, you feel your child's pain in the deepest part of yourself. You become the mother or father lion protecting your cubs. You roar and rage, hoping to scare the enemy away, and when that doesn't work you attack, willing to fight to the death to protect your young.

Divorce intensifies the feelings of responsibility and protection that most parents feel for their children, because the parenting partnership, with its daily support and reinforcement system, has been severed. In divorce you see your ex as the enemy, and in seeking to protect your cubs you attack the other parent. This fighting between parents actually leaves the children feeling unsafe and insecure. Their self-esteem wavers, and because they're programmed to be egocentric they often blame themselves for your fights. In addition, with their parents fighting, they feel that they have no one to turn to, which often results in them turning to their peers. An adult child of divorced parents recalls:

I remember when my parents got divorced. It was awful. First of all, I hadn't had a clue that it was going to happen, because my parents were always very private about their fighting. But when they got divorced, the fights suddenly became public. I remember my mother, whom I'd never heard scream before, yelling into the telephone at my father, only to burst into tears when she hung up. And when I stayed with my dad, all he could do was tell me how unreasonable a person my mother was and how much I needed his influence so I wouldn't grow up to be like her. I felt so helpless and lost. And this went on for years. When I was in my teens, I really relied on my peers for support. Unfortunately, at that time everyone was really into drugs and booze. To be a part of my peers, I did that stuff, too. I've been sober and drug free for years now, but I sure wish things had been different. I really feel like I wasted a lot of years because my mom and dad were so busy fighting over me that they forgot to give me the support and protection I needed.

OVERPROTECTING THEM

When we try to protect our children, we often err on the side of overprotection by doing things for them that they could do for themselves—including solving problems that they might have with their other parent. Overprotection is always to a child's detriment; it is seen by children as a sign that they can't handle things themselves, that they are incompetent, and that we don't have confidence in them. Overprotection diminishes self-esteem.

In a divorce, it's easy to take any issue or complaint that our child has with his other parent and snatch it up as our cause, waving it like a banner as we rush in to do battle. By taking over in this way, we actually put our children at a severe disadvantage. Not only do they wind up not knowing whom they can turn to when the issues they have cause Mom and Dad to fight, but they also lose out on the possibility of developing some very helpful problem-solving skills for themselves.

When you are loving and supportive and refrain from taking over the problems that your children have with their other parent, you help your children feel competent and secure in their relationships with both of you. On the other hand, trying to "fix" problems for your children makes them think to themselves, *Gee, I guess I can't handle things on my own. And with Mom and Dad fighting, things aren't so safe, either. If it's unsafe and I can't handle it, then there is nowhere to turn.*

With this in mind, it's not only essential to be able to identify when your child tops the problem pyramid; it's vital that you be well versed in the techniques that will help you support your child in solving his or her own problems.

LISTENING NEUTRALLY TO YOUR CHILD

Listening to your child, really listening, gives her the sense that what she has to say matters and is worthwhile, that she herself is worthwhile. When children feel listened to, they feel accepted. Think about how you feel when you talk to your best friend. Your best friend is probably your best friend because he or she listens to you. You feel accepted by your friend, and when you leave a conversation with him or her you feel better about yourself. Why? Because you felt heard and therefore accepted by this person. That feeling of acceptance builds the foundation for a close, healthy relationship.

REFRAINING FROM ACTING ON YOUR OWN FEELINGS

The first step in really listening to your child lies not in what you do but in what you stop yourself from doing. You must stop yourself from acting on your feelings. This may be especially difficult, because your child's feelings about something your ex did or said are likely to stir up negative feelings within you. When your feelings become engaged during a conversation with your child, remember that your child's feelings are not the same as yours. Stop yourself from taking on those feelings and becoming enraged in front of your child. Refrain from leaping out of your chair, running to the phone, dialing your ex, and screaming obscenities at him or her.

This is not to say that you must bury your feelings of anger. On the contrary, if your anger is denied in front of your child, either by covering it up ("I'm fine; nothing's wrong," said through gritted teeth while your eye is twitching) or outright lying about it ("No, honey, Mommy and Daddy aren't angry with each other; it's only a little disagreement"), your child will become confused. These statements of denial refute her own notion of reality, because children are very adept at picking up on other people's subtle (and not so subtle) feelings. Children who have to deny the reality they see learn to distrust their own feelings. They also stop trusting other people. In short, they will probably need years of psychotherapy in the future!

To get around this tricky issue, if your child picks up on your negative feelings and asks whether you're angry at your ex you can say something along the lines of, "I do feel a little angry; you're right. But it's okay for us both to have our own feelings. These feelings are normal." You can even add, "Just because people have angry or upset feelings, it doesn't make them bad people. All people feel angry sometimes, whether they're divorced or not." Remember that it's okay to have your feelings and to acknowledge them, just not to act on them.

LISTENING WITH HEART

In *The Little Prince,* by Antoine de Saint-Exupéry, the fox says, "It is only with the heart that one can see rightly. What is essential is invisible to the eye." When we "listen with heart" to our children, we open our hearts to what they have to say, even if it's not something we want to hear. We put aside our own agendas, priorities, and even feelings to hear what's at the core of their communication.

To do this, we must sit still, make eye contact, and take deep breaths that allow us to be fully present in the moment so that we can attempt to objectively hear what it is that our child is saying. This is not necessarily an easy process, both because children speak in "code" and because you may have feelings of your own as your child speaks.

CRACKING THE KIDS' CODE

The first thing to keep in mind as you're listening with heart to your child is that what he says is not necessarily what he means. For example: "I hate Daddy. I don't want to visit him anymore" may fit in nicely with your own wishes, but in all likelihood what your child is really saying is "I am frustrated because Daddy won't let me ___."

As you listen to your child, be careful that you don't project your own feelings into what he is saying. If you're angry at your ex, use caution in how you interpret your child's words—there's a difference between a child feeling disappointed, frustrated, or sad and him feeling angry or enraged. Your child should be allowed to feel whatever he feels, but remember that they're his feelings, not yours. When you adopt your child's feelings as your own or project your feelings onto your child, you only complicate matters.

Here's what one adult had to say about how it affected her when her mother projected her own feelings into the situation and acted upon them:

> Once, after a visit with my father, I was really disappointed because I felt like he hadn't paid enough attention to me when I was there. So I complained to my mom about the visit. The next thing I knew, she was screaming at him. I felt mortified. I felt like I had gotten my father in trouble. I stopped telling my mother things after that.

If you have difficulty listening neutrally when your child is talking, try pretending that he is talking about someone you don't know rather than about his other parent. Lean forward, incline your head slightly, keep your arms and legs uncrossed, and let your child know that you're listening non-judgmentally. Remember that if your child thinks you're criticizing your ex, he will do one of two things: He will either stop coming to you to discuss these problems like the woman in the preceding paragraph did with her mother, or he will become protective of the other parent. If your child feels that he has to defend his other parent, it will distort his feelings and confuse him. Your child might get the message that he is never allowed to be mad at his other parent because it leaves that parent unprotected.

Shielding one parent from the other is too big a job for a kid, no matter what his or her age. Stop yourself from putting your child in that position. Listen neutrally.

ACKNOWLEDGING

One thing that helps children feel listened to is when you restate what they've said in your own words. It's also helpful to interject a feeling word when you do this. In order to not inadvertently block communication, phrase your restatement in the following manner:

That must have been [difficult, hard, uncomfortable].

That sounds so [frustrating, frightening, sad].

Seems like you're [angry, unhappy, lonely].

I guess [it's difficult sometimes, you're feeling confused, your feelings are hurt].

Sometimes it's [upsetting, maddening, overwhelming].

What all these phrases have in common is that they convey an attitude of hesitation on your part. When you come on too strong, you take the risk of mislabeling your child's feelings. You don't want your children feeling obligated to take on emotions that don't belong to them.

> I remember when my parents split up. I was so sad. And my mother kept saying, "Aren't you angry at your dad?" After hearing this a thousand times, I actually *got* angry and didn't speak to my dad for years. It was a bad scene.

When you are hesitant in reflecting your child's feelings, you also leave room for your child to contradict or correct you. For example, suppose your child says, "I'm not going back to Mommy's house ever again." You might guess that your child feels angry and hesitantly reflect that feeling with, "Gee, you sound kind of angry." If you're wrong and your child is really feeling embarrassed, he has an opportunity to tell you that "no, I'm just embarrassed because I got chocolate on her new couch." When your child does contradict or correct you, it's important that you acknowledge the correction with, "Oh, I see; I was wrong. What you really felt was embarrassment."

When children are sorting through their feelings, they need to experiment with finding the right feeling word as well as deciding how strongly they feel, and it's important to allow them this self-discovery. For instance, if your son says, "I hate Daddy," you'll negate his feeling if you say, "No, you don't." Saying, out loud, that he hates his father is the way your son is able to express intense anger. Or he may be annoyed and frustrated at his father and is confusing those feelings with anger. Your goal is to simply rephrase, deemphasizing the word "hate" by saying, "Wow, you sure do sound angry." By allowing your child the space in which to explore different feelings and by validating these feelings, you will help your child eventually be able to express himself fully, not only to you but to your ex as well.

BRAINSTORMING WITH KIDS

After you've acknowledged to your child that you're listening by using appropriate body language and by restating what you heard her say, the next step is to turn the problem-solving process over to her. Most of us reached adulthood without ever mastering the skill of effectively solving interpersonal problems. Yet it is a skill that can open doors, bridge rivers, and launch people from mediocre to brilliant careers. The ability to problem-solve is a versatile gift that will last throughout your child's lifetime, one he will use in a variety of situations. Fortunately, too, if you help your child learn to solve her own problems, it lessens your contact with your ex and unburdens you.

Adults can help children look for solutions by asking a series of questions. The first question effectively leaves the solution in your child's hands. Phrase your first statement in this way: "Can you think of anything you might be able to do about that?"

From this basic foundation a variety of similar questions can be formed. Here are a few suggestions:

Is there any way you'd feel comfortable asking your dad about that?

Can you think of a way to turn this around?

I wonder what you might be able to do about this?

The key is that you must not include any suggestions or advice. For example, saying, "Well, I think you should tell your father to go f*** himself," is a terrible idea whether it's stated that way or in a more subtle manner like, "Why don't you tell your father that if he doesn't let you go out with your friends, you won't come over anymore." It's easy to insert our own agendas, advice, and solutions into our conversations with children, but it has far-reaching and potentially devastating effects. Even simple, neutral solutions, such as "Just go ask your dad to let you stay up later," will keep your child from learning to work things out on his own. Admittedly, providing solutions for your child rather than supporting him in working things out for himself is not going to put your child into therapy for the rest of his life. However, it's not going to give him the thinking skills he needs, either.

It's also very important that you don't criticize your child for thinking freely. Even if you know that a particular solution is impossible or impractical, let it ride for the time being. For example, if your child responds that she's going to pack her bags and move to Australia, you can say, "Packing your bag and moving to Australia is one solution. Can you think of another? I'd be very sad if you moved to Australia."

GIVING ADVICE CAREFULLY

When you've posed the initial question, your child may not be able to come up with any solutions or may be able to come up only with ones that you know aren't feasible. Then it's appropriate for you to offer some solutions of your own. This is a bit tricky, however, for a couple of reasons. First of all, it's easy to allow your own bias and need for revenge to creep in and to offer advice that is prejudiced. Clearly this is a mistake and does more harm than not helping your child at all. The second thing that makes offering advice tricky is that, as with adults, giving unsolicited advice blocks communication with our children, which is the opposite of what we're trying to do here.

WONDERING WHAT WOULD HAPPEN IF . . .

To offer advice without blocking communication, phrase it as if you're exploring possible solutions to the problem. Instead of saying, "Why don't you . . . ," or, "I think you should . . . ," say, "I wonder what would happen if you. . . ." Like the initial question you pose to your child, this question serves as a launching pad for similar questions that will get your child thinking about possible solutions. Here are a few more suggestions:

I wonder what would happen if you talked to your dad about this?

What do you think your mom would do if you . . . ?

I wonder if ___ would work?

Have you thought about . . . ?

Remember that whenever you offer advice, state it in question form, not only to keep the lines of communication open but for a higher purpose as well. If done correctly, this process increases your child's confidence in her ability to problem-solve. Because she was not forced into a position of expressly taking your advice (after all, you asked her what she thought would happen if she took a particular action), she is more likely to take credit if a solution is found. Nevermind if that solution came from you in the first place—you don't need the credit for it; you're an adult. If you allow her to take credit she can more confidently handle future issues not only with your ex but also with friends, family members, teachers, and others.

HANDLING NEGATIVITY

It is naïve to assume that this process works as smoothly in life as it does on paper. In fact, more likely than not, once you state your initial question, "Can you think of anything you might be able to do about that?" your child will say, "No! There's nothing I can do." Likewise, if you proceed undaunted, your child will probably reject all of the solutions you pose. This is to be expected. When this rejection happens (note we don't say "if" it happens), accept your child's feelings. You can say things like:

You sound pretty hopeless.

Sometimes it's hard to talk to your dad [mom].

Mmm, I guess you think that wouldn't work—sometimes it's hard to come up with an idea.

It's also important to add encouragement with words like:

I'm sure if we put our heads together we'll think of something.

You're good at coming up with solutions, and I feel confident you'll figure out a way to handle this to your satisfaction.

It's important to note that this process is not about results and coming up with solutions. It's about establishing, maintaining, and enriching your relationship with your child. This is a point to be repeated and emphasized. (If we could, we'd lean forward, look intently into your eyes, and gesture emphatically!)

This process is not about results.
It's about enriching your relationship with your child!

If you become involved in solving the problem, the problem-solving process won't work. It sounds like a contradiction, but it's not. It's true that if you stay in the process, it's likely that you'll achieve a result, but that's not the primary goal. We'll repeat it one more time: The goal is to enrich your relationship with your child so that she feels listened to, protected, and supported by you. Keep your relationship with your child, even if your child has negative feelings about you or your ex, in the foreground of this process.

EXAMINING CONSEQUENCES

Part of problem solving and making "good" decisions involves being able to look at the choices you might be making and what will happen if those choices are implemented. As you know, the results of our choices are called consequences. When your child tops the problem pyramid and you engage in listening and supporting him or her in solving a problem, you help your child examine the consequences to the solutions he or she comes up with. Taking your children seriously and helping them explore the ramifications of their decisions ultimately helps them make the best choices they can. For example, if your child says, "I'm never going to Dad's house again!" help him examine the consequences of that particular choice (even if you know it's an empty threat). You could say, "Well, how do you think you would feel about that?" or, "Well, that's one solution. What do you think would happen if you never went there again?"

LETTING IT REST

Sometimes questions that help your child examine the consequences of a particular action are met with a response that either is impractical, can't be implemented, or both: "If I never stay with my dad again, I'd feel great. I hate him and his dumb old wife anyway. So I'm never going again." Rather than jumping for joy or, conversely, trying to convince your child why she can't choose that, simply let it rest. You can acknowledge her feeling without agreeing: "Well, let's continue to talk about this. I still sense that you're very angry, and maybe we can figure out a way for you not to feel so angry anymore." It's important to realize that many times a child needs to reject an idea in order to save face and she will come around very soon afterward.

ALLOWING YOUR CHILD TO HAVE A RELATIONSHIP WITH THE OTHER PARENT

No matter how you feel about your ex, your child must develop his own relationship with his other parent. This is not an easy process, because you can rest assured that your child has many mixed feelings about your ex. Your child may blame your ex for the divorce, may resent a new relationship that is developing between your ex and another person, undoubtedly feels sad, abandoned, and angry, and probably feels confused about how to have a relationship with two parents who no longer live together.

Allowing your child to develop this relationship, to make mistakes and to achieve successes that are all his own, while still supporting and struggling to understand things from his point of view, is a great gift. So if you feel yourself wanting to intervene, give advice, put down or roll your eyes at a solution your child comes up with, stop. Sometimes your intervention causes more problems. And it almost always confuses matters.

Allowing your ex and your child to develop their own relationship might also mean not covering for your ex. Sometimes an ex really isn't a very good parent, and all the manipulation you exert won't necessarily keep your child from finding that out. You won't want to make a point of telling your child something that might hurt him, but don't lie if your child asks about it:

My ex and I were back in court after being divorced for many years because he was seeking a downward modification of child support. It seemed that his salary just didn't go far enough now that he had a new wife and family. Anyway, he said that he didn't want our son to spend the night anymore, at least until a new child support agreement was signed. Well, the last thing I wanted was to involve Eric in all of this. So instead of telling him, I arranged for him to have something special to do on the weekends he was supposed to see his dad. This went on for about three months before Eric finally asked what was going on and why he wasn't sleeping at his dad's house anymore. Then it hit me. I should have given my son more credit. Looking back, I realized that it was only a matter of time before my son would figure it out. I also decided that my son deserves honest answers from me. It preserves our trust and helps him know he can always count on me to tell him the truth. So I explained that his dad had asked that we curtail the weekend visitation until a new child support agreement was signed. I didn't embellish; I didn't let my anger show; I simply told him the facts.

HANDLING AFTERSHOCKS AHEAD OF TIME

The emphasis in this chapter has been on supporting your child in handling issues with your ex, rather than taking over and making your child's problem your problem. But this doesn't mean stepping out of the picture entirely. After all, you do have the advantage of having a longer history with your ex than your child does. Sometimes this enables you to predict how your ex might react in a particular situation with your child.

Your knowledge of your ex's personality can go a long way

toward helping your child come up with the best solution to a particular problem. Don't state that you know what the outcome might be with a negative phrase like, "Oh, forget it! Your mom will never go for that. She'll just explode at you and you'll wind up right back where you are now, but with more hurt feelings." Rather, use your information to explore further consequences: "Well, you could do that. [Pause.] How do you think your mom will react? How would you go about telling her about your decision?"

It's important to try to work through as much of the proposed scenario as possible ahead of time. If you know that your ex is likely to be explosive, uncooperative, or simply nonresponsive, yet your child doesn't respond to your questions with, "Well, I guess Dad would really blow his cool and yell at me" (or whatever you know your ex is likely to do), it's important to suggest gently to the child what you think might happen. Again, hesitation on your part creates the impression that you're not trying to be a know-it-all and that you're not against your ex. You might try saying something like, "Well, I have a feeling Mom might respond pretty strongly to this. What do you think?"

HANDLING MANIPULATION

Like the history that exists between you and your ex, there is a history between you and your child and between your child and your ex. Be aware that your child is very conscious of the different dynamics that exist. Your child may know that you're the "soft" one, the one who gives her what she wants, or that your ex is. Sometimes this means that your child may try to manipulate you into handling the problem for her. Please understand that we don't intend the term "manipulate" to be entirely negative. All human beings are manipulative at some time or another. It doesn't mean that your child is "bad." What it means is that your child is likely to figure out the easiest route to get what she wants. Your child may see that the easiest route involves playing one parent off the other, and sometimes she will see that it's easier to get you to argue her case for her with your ex.

It's very important to give your child the confidence to confront your ex, since she will have to deal with her other parent for the rest of her life. If you allow yourself to be manipulated into taking on your child's problem, you will, in fact, diminish your child's self-confidence and self-esteem. Your child will feel as though she needs you to rescue her, which only sets her up to remain in a helpless role. So when you see your child trying to get you to take over a problem that clearly doesn't belong to you, gently reflect how she must be feeling back to her. Say, "Sounds like you're a little anxious about talking to your dad. I can tell you'd really like me to step in."

To boost your child's confidence, have confidence in yourself and convey that confidence to your child. Say, "This is something you can handle yourself. Let's see if we can find a way to make you feel more comfortable when you do." By phrasing it this way, you make it known to your child that you think she can do it, whether she feels comfortable or not. This kind of confidence goes a long way in supporting children in solving their own problems.

WHEN YOUR CHILD'S PROBLEM IS WITH YOU

Children often become angry with us because as parents, we're in the position of authority. As such, you may need to set limits or boundaries that your children will not necessarily like. Setting those boundaries is a central topic in numerous parenting books. This issue, however, applies to parents in joint custody situations when the child says, "I hate you. I'm packing my toys and I'm going to live with Mommy." In this statement, it is clear that the child is topping the problem pyramid, but because his problem is with you it can be tricky to handle. Here are the steps:

1. **Listen neutrally:** This is difficult when you feel insulted, threatened, and fearful that your child might actually choose to go live with your ex. Remember that children speak in code and just because they're threatening you, it doesn't mean that they actually want to take action. Refuse to be upset, and listen objectively.

2. **Show concern:** Restate what you think your child is saying. Try to determine how he is feeling by watching his body language, listening to his words and tone of voice, and observing his facial expressions. Put

yourself in his shoes. How would you feel if it were you? Use feeling words ("sad," "confused," "angry") to show him that you're concerned and that you understand his feelings: "It's so hard sometimes, isn't it? It must be a little confusing, too. On the one hand, you're so angry and so hurt that you are threatening to go live with your dad. On the other hand, you love me. That can be difficult."

3. **Brainstorm solutions:** Let your child know that most topics are open for some discussion. If he can think of anything that would make things easier, he should let you know. "Honey, what can we do about this? I see you seem really mad at me. Maybe if we discussed it, we could come up with a solution together."

4. **Let go:** Let go, let go, let go, let go, let go. Disengage your feelings. Recognize the difficulty your child must be having. Try not to feel threatened. If you refuse to be hurt and maintain a calm, supportive attitude, your child will eventually wind down and be able to think more clearly. Your child can't hurt you if you don't accept the hurt. Let it go.

THE PRE-VERBAL CHILD

A discussion about what to do when your child has a problem wouldn't be complete without mentioning the pre-verbal child. As any parent of a pre-verbal child who's throwing a tantrum can attest, children don't have to have language to have problems. Of course, the challenge for parents of a toddler or infant is that you don't necessarily know, nor will you necessarily ever find out, what the problem actually is. This doesn't mean, however, that you're off the hook. It is just as important, if not more important in many ways, that you acknowledge the feelings your little ones may be having.

Because they're not capable of expressing themselves verbally, very young children usually express themselves physically, especially in the case of strong emotions such as fear, anger, confusion, and frustration. Your otherwise placid and adorable toddler may hit, bite, scream, and kick when he is feeling a particularly strong emotion. And make no mistake, young children feel the anger and turbulence between you and your ex just as acutely as older children do.

When addressing pre-verbal children regarding a problem they are having, be attuned to the ways an emotion is likely to manifest itself. In other words, watch for their feelings more than listen for them. Here are some things to look for.

Facial Expression

Children may frown, grind their teeth, suck their thumbs or fingers, tense their mouths, clench their teeth, or close their eyes instead of looking at you. By watching your child's facial expression and thinking to yourself what it would mean if you made the same expression, you can draw clues that will help you interpret what your child is feeling.

Body Language

Pre-verbal children who have a problem may avert their gaze, cry, tense their bodies, or clench their fists. They may also become aggressive: biting, hitting, pinching, scratching, kicking, or banging their heads. Body language is a good external indicator of internal emotion.

Tone of Voice

Listen for pitch and volume. Even without words, tone of voice can indicate strong emotion. Pitch may go up and volume may increase if a child is particularly distressed. Volume may decrease if a child is withdrawing. By watching the pre-verbal child's emotional indicators you can make some pretty good guesses about underlying feelings. And even though your child is pre-verbal, it is important to verbalize to her what you think her feelings are. (Do this even if she's only a couple of months old. After all, even newborns have feelings!)

When you reflect your pre-verbal child's feelings, it helps the child learn the words she will eventually use to express her emotions. Even children as young as two have learned the word "frustrated" and are capable of using it properly. In addition, you show your child (through your tone of voice more than the words you use) that someone is calm and in control. Children who are having strong feelings about something, especially if they're having trouble expressing those feelings, need a parent who seems calm and in control more than anything else. This gives the child a feeling of safety. You might say things like,

"You seem sad," "I guess you're upset about Daddy going back to his house," "Sounds like something happened that you're frustrated about."

Even though these seem like a lot of words for children who aren't using words themselves, it's important to keep in mind that children understand adults long before they're able to express themselves verbally. While a little empathy goes a long way for the pre-verbal child, don't think you have to stop there. It's perfectly all right, and even desirable, to continue with the technique and wonder aloud whether there is anything that would help the child feel better or differently. Remember that this process is not about results. It's about enriching your relationship with your child! (Sound familiar?) And if nothing else, you're getting the practice that you'll need when your child does begin to talk!

ONIONS IN THE TUNA

Let's look at a situation between Caitlin and her father. You'll see that Mom originally responds to Caitlin's problem by taking over but later helps Caitlin solve it herself:

Caitlin was so hungry when she got home from camp the other day, she didn't even say hello before heading for the kitchen. She had spent the night before at her dad's, and at first I thought it was just a readjustment thing. Then as I watched her grab a bag of chips and disappear into her room, I looked in her lunch bag. She had taken one bite out of the

sandwich her dad had made for her and left the rest un-
touched. As I inspected the sandwich, I saw that the tuna
he had made was riddled with raw onions. I went nuts, because I know that Caitlin hates onions. I called him up and
started screaming at him, asking him how he could make
a sandwich like that for a six-year-old. And you know what
he said? He said that in his house he makes tuna with onions and that she would have to learn to like it. He makes
me furious. We ended up hanging up on each other.

The first mistake that Caitlin's mom, Marianne, makes here
is in assuming that onions in the tuna are a problem for Caitlin.
Although Mom might suspect this is the case, it's also possible
that Caitlin simply wasn't hungry at lunchtime. Remember that
when we make assumptions—even if we believe we can't possibly be wrong—we often create problems that wouldn't have
existed otherwise. Before you address a problem that your child
may be having, ask him or her if it is actually a problem.

The second mistake that Marianne makes is rushing in to
solve the problem on Caitlin's behalf. As you can see, Marianne's
intervention started another fight with her ex and, quite possibly,
caused him to take an extreme stand (that Caitlin would just
have to learn to like tuna with onions) that he might not otherwise have taken.

Let's see what happens the following week:

Caitlin was fine until I mentioned that she should pack to go
to her dad's house that night. Then I noticed that she became

rather lethargic and started to complain about a stomach-ache. We went back and forth for a while, and finally she told me that she didn't want to go to her dad's house because he cooked "weird" things for dinner and put onions in her tuna.

When children have a problem that's unresolved, they usually bring it up in some way. If Marianne had waited instead of calling her ex, the situation would still have come to light. Of course, Marianne's first impulse was to call her ex again, find out what he was cooking for dinner, and remind him that Caitlin would not eat onions. But this time, she tried a different tack. She began by reflecting Caitlin's feelings:

"Sounds like you're not real happy about what your dad has to eat at his house."

"Mom, I hate onions. Do I have to go?"

"I wonder if you can think of any way you might talk to your dad about that."

"I don't want to. He might get mad."

"Well, he might. I wonder if we could figure out a way to talk about it with him so he doesn't?"

"Well, how would I do that?"

"Hmmm, what do you think would happen if you used an 'I' statement?" (Yes, we're advocating that you teach your child the very techniques we're teaching you in this book.) "Maybe you could say something like, 'Dad, I feel upset because I don't like onions.' And what could you ask him for instead?"

"Maybe he could make me peanut butter."

"There you go! So what if you said, 'Dad, I feel upset because

I don't like onions. Could you please make me a peanut butter sandwich instead?' Do you think you'd feel comfortable trying it that way?"

"Okay."

When Caitlin called her dad, the conversation went something like this:

> *Hi, Daddy. I'm coming over tonight, right? . . . What are you making for dinner? . . . You know what I really like? I like it when you make macaroni and cheese. Could I please have that tonight? . . . No, I don't like lamb chops. I like macaroni and cheese. That's all I want, macaroni and cheese. And Daddy, could I please have peanut butter and jelly for lunch tomorrow? Will you make that for me, please? I can even help you make it tonight? . . . Yeah, I really like peanut butter and jelly . . . and macaroni and cheese. Thanks, Daddy.*

While this wasn't exactly the way in which Marianne and Caitlin had worked it out, Marianne had clearly given Caitlin the tools she needed to feel confident talking to her dad about the problem.

WHAT TO DO WHEN YOUR CHILD TOPS THE PROBLEM PYRAMID

Let's look at some examples where your child tops the problem pyramid and work through them step-by-step.

Packing Problems

My ex never bothers to repack my daughter's clothes, school-work and games, and she always makes a big scene when she returns home and realizes that she's missing things. I'm really tired of buying her new stuff because her dad can't remember to pack her things.

What is the problem here?

My daughter's things are never returned to my house.

All of her things? And they are never returned?

Okay. Some of my daughter's things were missing when she came home last time and she was upset. This happens frequently. *[Remember to change your language to keep things in the present and not generalize with "always" and "never." It keeps your issues in perspective, and your feelings will be less intense.]*

Who tops the problem pyramid?

Who has the upset feelings? Mother and daughter.

Who's bringing up the issue? Daughter.

Who is responsible for implementing the solution? Daughter.

The daughter is responsible for implementing the solution because her name appears as the answer to the first two questions.

A different father or mother however, might decide that he or she owns the problem. Maybe another child wouldn't care that schoolwork is being left. But in either case, the solution lies in empowering the child to take responsibility for his or her belongings. Let's see how that's done:

The daughter has just returned home, discovered that she's missing her favorite doll, and begins to cry. (We've included the steps of the communication process to help break it down for you.)

1. **Listen:** Mom gets down on one knee, looks the child in the eye, and says, "Honey, what's wrong? You seem so upset."

   "I left my doll at Daddy's. He didn't pack my doll!"

2. **Show concern:** "That's hard. I know how you love that doll."

   "I want my doll. Please will you go get it for me, please?"

   "Mmm, you'd like me to go back and get it, huh? I don't think there's time for that today, honey."

   "But I can't sleep without my doll. Daddy never remembers anything. Please, please go get her for me?"

3. **"Can you think of anything . . . ?"** "I know you're really upset, honey. Can you think of any way you

might be able to handle this yourself, because I won't have time to go back today."

"No! Please? I need her today."

4. "I wonder what would happen if . . . ?"

"I wonder what would happen if you called your dad and asked him to bring the doll later tonight?"

"I can't! Daddy will get mad at me."

"Well, can you think of any way you can get along without her until tomorrow?"

"Nooooo!"

"I know, honey. Maybe what we need to do here is figure out how you can best remember to pack your own toys and things so you won't have to go a night without them?"

"If you'll go get my dolly tonight, I promise I'll remember to pack her next time."

"I'm glad you want to take responsibility for packing her next time. Let's figure out a way to help you remember, and I'll go and pick her up tomorrow."

This parent is on the right track. She has set a firm limit to teach responsibility (her daughter loses the doll for one night, which will help her remember to pack it next time). In addition, the mother doesn't allow her daughter to blame her father for forgetting to pack the doll because she realizes that it will be to her daughter's benefit in the long run to take that responsibility herself. Mom also recognizes that her daughter is developmentally capable of remembering her own things and opens the door to the process of brainstorming solutions to help her remember her things in the future.

Next, Mom addresses the current issue with a limit (she won't jump in to fix the situation by going to get the doll tonight) but shows a willingness to figure out ways to help her daughter handle that limit for the night. Although no immediate solution was reached, Mom remembered that this process is about enriching her relationship with her child as well as teaching her daughter responsibility. She was patient as well as confident that they could handle this together. She didn't blame or allow her child to blame her father, which would only set Mom up for possible manipulation in the future.

Text Trouble

It's bad enough that my teenage daughter is forever on her phone, texting her friends, but on the weekends she spends with me I see her become visibly upset because her mom has texted her about something. Often it's about how much she misses her, and sometimes it's about cleaning her room. I've asked my ex to leave us alone on "my" time, but she just ignores this and calls, texts, or IMs at will.

What is the problem here?

Nicole is upset when her mother texts her on "our" time.

Who tops the problem pyramid? Who has the upset feelings?

Nicole.

Who brought up the issue?

Nicole, though perhaps not verbally. Remember that body language is even more important than verbal communication. Nicole's being visibly upset counts as bringing up the issue.

Who is responsible for implementing the solution?

Nicole. (Although it should be noted that it appears Dad has a problem with Nicole being "forever on the phone," which may intensify his feelings about seeing Nicole upset when her mother texts her. It's important for Dad to separate the problems, and if he decides that he's frustrated with Nicole's texting, regardless of whether or not it's her mother on the other end, then he should identify himself as topping the problem pyramid and take that up as a separate issue with Nicole.)

What are your most intense feelings?

I feel frustrated that my time with Nicole is interrupted by her mother's neediness and that an otherwise pleasant weekend is destroyed because Nicole is upset.

What thoughts are causing those feelings?

Nicole's mother is so needy and enmeshed. She can't let Nicole alone for a minute and she constantly tries to weasel in on Nicole's relationship with me.

Let's see how the communication between Dad and Nicole might work. Nicole receives a text and looks visibly upset.

1. Listen: "Nicole, honey, I see you're upset. What's up?"

    "Nothing. It's just Mom again."

    "Mom's texting you again?" (This is just a restatement of what Nicole has just said, not an accusation.)

    "Yeah."

2. Show concern: "Hmmm . . . it seems like it sometimes upsets you that she texts you when you're here." (Note that Dad kept the incident in the present by saying "sometimes" rather than saying "it upsets you that she texts you . . .")

    "Yeah, sometimes."

3. "Can you think of anything . . . ?" "Can you think of a way you might be able to tell your mom that?"

    "No. She'd just get even more upset. I don't want to hurt her feelings."

    "You don't want to hurt her feelings. I understand that. Can you think of a way to tell her that wouldn't hurt her feelings?"

    "I don't know. Like what?"

4. "What do you think would happen if . . . ?"

    "Well, what do you think would happen if you said, 'Mom, I love you, too, and I enjoy texting with you. I'm in the middle of something right now; how about if I text you when I'm done?'"

"I don't know, Dad. I mean, I'm not really in the middle of something. That would kind of be a lie."

"Hmmm. I hear your concern."

"Yeah. I mean, it just seems like whenever we're watching TV or something she always texts me."

"So when you're in the middle of something she texts you."

"Yeah."

"Well, honey, I hate to see you upset. If you think of any way I can be helpful, let me know, okay?"

"Okay. Thanks Dad."

This is a nice conversation in a couple of respects. First, Dad doesn't try to fix the problem. He simply uses the conversation to express empathy and build his relationship with his daughter. Second, he never accuses her mother of interrupting their time. Third, even though Dad presents a possible solution (that Nicole could text her mom to say she's in the middle of something), he doesn't point out, later in the conversation, that even though Nicole turned that solution down as a "lie," she actually does feel interrupted.

While it may initially seem as though Dad has made no headway at all, the truth is that he's left the door open for future problem solving. Interestingly, several weeks later Nicole reopened the issue:

"Oh Dad? You remember how we were talking about Mom texting me all the time when I'm here?"

"Mmm-hmmm."

"Well, I told her that I liked talking to her and texting her, but I said I'd rather that we talk right before bed because it wasn't always easy to get to my phone during the day."

"Wow! It sounds like you came up with a great solution. I know you wondered if she would have hurt feelings—how did she respond?"

"Oh, she was fine after all."

"Great, I'm glad you worked it out."

STAYING OUT OF IT

Allowing children to fight their own battles is one of the hardest parenting skills to learn. Our inclination is to jump in the ring with our child, help him fight the "enemy" or accomplish the job, protect him from harm, and celebrate victory with him afterward. But children need to learn how to do things themselves. Just as a two-year-old shouts, "Me-do-it," children fare better when they are guided and taught to solve problems and finish projects by themselves. Once you learn that many of the problems your children are having belong to them and you support them in solving those problems for themselves, your relationship with your children and with your ex will improve.

Keep in mind that we're not suggesting that you leave your children to fend for themselves in a dangerous situation. Nor are we saying that you should ask children to solve problems that are above their developmental capacity to handle. Rather, we're suggesting that you think through the problems that come up for your children and thoughtfully assess their ability to solve these problems.

Whenever possible, empower your child or children with the communication and problem-solving skills that will raise their self-esteem. Giving them the courage to talk to their other parent is a gift. It will enrich their lives and deepen their capacity for healthy relationships.

8.

Empowering Your Child

EMPOWERMENT = SELF-ESTEEM

There is no question that most children of divorce suffer. One day, the world as they know it changes on them. One parent may move out, or they themselves may need to move. Many of the family's rules, from one day to the next, have changed. Their stable and familiar world suddenly feels unsafe and uncontrollable.

We're not saying this to make you feel guilty. In fact, there is good evidence that children whose parents fight all the time and still stay together may be harmed more than those whose parents divorced. But it's important to know that when you divorce, and especially if you think your ex is a jerk, your child's self-esteem and self-confidence can suffer greatly.

When we talk about empowering your child, we're really talking about building your child's self-esteem so that he feels good about himself. An empowered child is one who cooperates, has high self-esteem, can be flexible, and thrives—even in difficult situations. When children feel good about themselves, they are more resilient, capable, and resourceful. When children's self-esteem is high, they are willing to try harder, reach out to others, and learn from the mistakes they make. Children who have high self-esteem are less likely to misbehave and are more capable of examining choices and determining which choices are appropriate.

On the other hand, if a child's self-esteem is low, she is less likely to reach out to others for support. Many children with low self-esteem do dangerous or risky things. They're less capable of handling the effects of divorce on their lives. They're more likely to give up, stop trying, and misbehave. In addition, children who feel bad about themselves, who feel they lack power and control, are more likely to succumb to negative peer pressure.

Numerous things influence a child's self-esteem. How we discipline and communicate with our child, the things peers and other people say and do to our child, and the way our child affects the world around him all contribute to self-esteem. While you can't do much about the way other people interact with your child, you can certainly do something about how you handle your own child. Let's take a look at some esteem-building techniques.

A WORD ABOUT DISCIPLINE

We empower our children when we discipline them in a consistent way using respectful, limit-setting techniques. If you aren't consistent in your discipline, if you are reasoning with or spanking your child as your primary disciplinary tools, we urge you to find a workshop in your area that will help you learn to discipline in a loving, respectful, and firm way.

Setting limits for your child increases his or her feelings of safety and security, and how you set them affects your child's self-esteem. Setting them in a respectful way with related consequences increases your child's self-esteem and setting them in an hysterical, spur-of-the-moment, or unthoughtful way affects your child adversely. Children of divorce are especially vulnerable in this area. They need you to know what you're doing.

UNCONDITIONAL LOVE

The most important component in your child's self-esteem involves the words you use and actions you take that communicate your unconditional love for her. They are the words and actions you use when you discipline (that's why you need to learn limit-setting techniques). They are the words and actions you use when teaching children to tie their shoelaces, make their bed, or ride a bike. They are the casual, as well as the formal, words you use every day to communicate your feelings, wants, and needs. Saying, "I love you," isn't enough to make your child feel unconditionally loved.

In order to understand how to formulate your communication so that the underlying message is one of love, you must first understand why this is sometimes difficult to do.

HUMAN BEING VERSUS HUMAN DOING

When we love our children for who they are, no matter what they do, and communicate this love in very specific ways, we build a foundation for self-esteem that lasts through all the ups and downs that our children encounter throughout their lives.

When your child was born and you first held him in your arms, you probably felt a rush of love unlike any you had ever felt before. There was a bond between you and your child that was based solely on the fact that he existed, on his being. He didn't have to do anything or say anything for you to feel this incredible, overwhelming love. This feeling is what Carl Rogers, the renowned psychologist, calls unconditional positive regard, or unconditional love, and it is the foundation of positive self-esteem.

Feeling and expressing this love is relatively easy when our children are infants. After all, aside from keeping us up at night, they don't really do anything to anger, disappoint, or sadden us. We love them because they came into being. In fact, at this age they are pure "beings."

The difficulty arises when our "beings" start "doing" stuff: writing on the walls with Magic Marker, talking back, being nasty to their siblings. When they start doing things that we don't like, we begin to confuse who our children are (their being) with what they do (their doing.)

When children feel they have to earn our love by what they accomplish, they never feel good about themselves, no matter how much they do, no matter what their age. Indeed, some adults work outrageous hours, make huge salaries, and always strive to accomplish more and yet are never satisfied, no matter what they have achieved. This is because they were never given the free, unconditional love of their parents, the love that is every child's birthright.

Conveying unconditional love to your child, like everything else, isn't always easy. After all, the world judges your child and expects her to behave in a certain way. And there's no question that it's your job to teach your children to behave according to social norms. Add to that the reality that it's much easier to show unconditional love to a human being when she's not doing anything wrong and you have a complicated situation.

Showing your child that you love her unconditionally even when she misbehaves means learning specific techniques that separate who the child is from what the child does. For example, if your child spills a glass of milk and you say, "That was stupid! Couldn't you see that the milk would spill if you left it there?" it conveys to your child that he or she is stupid rather than that he or she made a mistake from which he or she can learn. Remember that "you" statements are accusatory and often attack the person's ego or "being." When you attack who your child is, not only do you increase the likelihood of defensiveness, you also damage his or her self-esteem.

Rather than "you" statements, "I" statements are helpful when you have to correct a child's behavior, because they effectively separate your feelings about the behavior from your feelings about the child. When you say, "I feel concerned when the milk is left close to the edge of the table because it could get accidentally knocked over. Please move it to the middle of the table," your child hears you setting a limit, not attacking who he is. Similarly, if the milk has actually spilled and you say, "I'm frustrated about the milk spilling; please clean it up," your child hears that he made a mistake that you would like him to correct. He doesn't hear that he's a bad person or that he does stupid things.

LISTENING TO YOUR CHILD

Listening to your child is a crucial part of building her self-esteem. Children (actually all people) who feel listened to come away believing that what they had to say was worthwhile and that they contributed to the communication. That makes them feel good about themselves.

Listening also has the potential to communicate to your child that you unconditionally love him or her. Quite often, children blame themselves for the divorce and feel that something they did, felt, or thought caused their parents to separate. They also get confused about their anger at one or both parents and may feel guilty for being angry. When you listen to your child and accept his feelings, however positive or negative those feelings are, you send the message to your child that you unconditionally love him.

If you could hear your child's thoughts, they might be something like this: "Wow, even though I feel terrible and angry and really upset, Dad didn't criticize me or give me advice.

He just listened. I think he really heard me. I think he must really love me to accept these awful feelings I have."

SHOWING CONFIDENCE

Another important criterion for children's self-esteem is how confident you are that they'll succeed—about both the things you ask of them (behaviorally) as well as the things the world expects. When you act as if you believe that your child is capable of handling situations as they arise, you build your child's confidence. Yet very often we inadvertently send the message that we expect our children not to succeed, at either life tasks or appropriate behavior. This message is conveyed when you say things like, "Don't forget your homework," or, "Be careful with that." What your child hears you say is, "I expect you to forget your homework," and, "I expect you to behave carelessly or recklessly." One dad told this story:

> I was up on a ladder pruning a tree in my yard last year and my neighbor came up to me and said, "Be careful; don't fall." I paused for a moment and thought, *What does she think I'm trying to do . . . intentionally fall off the ladder?*

When you hear these words said to an adult, you realize how ridiculous they are and you dismiss them as well-intentioned. Yet people use them all the time with children. The problem is that they rob children of their confidence in themselves. In essence, they communicate, "I expect you to be careless and fall off the ladder." Children, rather than dismissing this as an adult might do, are more likely to take it in and think, *Wow, I guess I'm careless.*

To show children that you have positive expectations about their behavior, phrase your statements in a more positive way. You might say, "I bet you felt proud that you remembered your homework yesterday. I know that you're working hard at being responsible for it every day." Likewise, instead of saying, "Be careful," try saying, "I saw how carefully you took your plate to the kitchen after dinner." By phrasing these statements positively and pointing to your child's sense of accomplishment, you give your child a feeling of confidence. When children feel confident about their abilities, they are less likely to make mistakes, to be careless, or to forget things.

This same principle works on adults, too, and even your ex. When you turn "don't forget . . ." into "remember to . . . ," it takes some of the sting out of it. See the difference when you say, "Please remember to pack Steph's ballet clothes," rather than, "Don't forget to pack Jason's baseball mitt."

LETTING GO OF IDEALS

Another way we unintentionally rob our children of their inner strength, and likewise their power, is by clinging to an "ideal" image of them. This image is what we expect our child to be: brave, honorable, loving, beautiful or handsome, good at math, athletic, and so on.

For most of us, the image building began before our child

was ever born and this "fantasy child" is usually based on our own childhood. Perhaps you always wanted to be a football hero or a ballet dancer but were never allowed to play ball or take ballet lessons. Maybe you were teased for being taller or heavier than your peers. Perhaps you always envied your brother, who was more athletic than you and excelled at sports.

All of our wishes and unfulfilled dreams, as well as our negative experiences with parents, siblings, and others, go into the creation of what we want our child to be, our "ideal" image of him or her. We'd like him to play football; we worry if she's heavier than her classmates; we wish that he were taller so he won't be teased; we push her in math so she can excel in college and "make something of herself."

Unfortunately, this idealization sends a message to our children that we have very high standards for them, standards they may never be able to live up to. They hear (sometimes without our even saying a word): "You'll never get it right; there will always be something wrong." Of course, we don't mean it that way. We're really trying to help our children be the best they can be. Nevertheless, the message is a negative one.

WATCHING OUT FOR "BUT"

Accepting our children as they are—fat, thin, tall, short, athletic, or artistic—is not easy to do. The words we use in everyday conversations convey to our children that there are things we don't accept about them. One of the words to catch yourself using and eliminate from your communication is the word "but."

When you say, "I like how you colored that, but you got a little out of the lines here," you inadvertently tell your child that he is not living up to your ideal image of him. This happens because the word "but" negates everything that came before it. Your child hears your perfectionism: "It's not quite right. Keep in the lines next time." Even if you believe you are delivering a compliment by saying, "You got a good grade in English this time, but your math needs improvement," your child essentially hears only what came after the "but"—"your math needs improvement"—and he or she will then add the unspoken but implied second half of the message, which is *and you need improvement, too.*

SEPARATING COMPLIMENTS FROM REQUESTS

To eliminate the word "but" from your vocabulary, separate sentences with the word "and" or with a period. For example, saying, "I see you got off to a good start cleaning your room and I know you'll be finished in no time," has a completely different effect from saying, "I see you got off to a good start cleaning your room, *but* you have a ways to go."

Another way to do this is to separate compliments from requests for behavioral change with a few minutes of time. When you tell your child, "Great job cleaning your room," end there. If you must go on to say, "There are a few toys you still need to put away," let the child take in the compliment fully and have it work toward empowering her. Then say, "Let me help you with the last few toys." In this way, you still draw her attention to the toys left out, just not in a way that criticizes her.

SEPARATING BEHAVIOR FROM LOVE

In order to further clarify for your child that you love him, even if he makes a mistake, be sure to separate your child's behavior from your love for him when you give him a compliment. Instead of saying, "What a good boy you are for cleaning your room," say, "I see you cleaned up your room."

All of us want to tell our children how terrific they are, and we should—frequently!—just not in conjunction with their behavior. Children should feel loved because they exist, not because they've behaved in a certain way. So instead of saying, "Wow! Great report card," hugging your child, and following it immediately with, "I love you," separate the two. Say, "I see you got A's in most of your subjects this time. I know you worked hard." Later you can say, "I love you," when your child is not doing anything other than just being himself.

Many parents have trouble believing that their child will continue to strive and do her best if they relax and stop watching her every moment along the way. Yet that's exactly what will happen. You must trust that what children need is your unconditional love and acceptance, even if they're having a hard time behaving. And sometimes the most important thing you can do is get out of your child's way and allow her just to be herself.

By letting go of your "ideal child" you'll free him to grow in healthy directions because he feels unconditionally accepted by you. Mourn the loss of this ideal child if you must, but convey to your child every day that you love him for who he is, not what he does. And trust that your child is trying to be the best he can be and that he will do this more readily without your criticism. Know that he usually sees his own faults without you continually pointing them out.

NOT VALIDATING THE "MONSTERS"

Another way we disempower our children and rob them of their self-esteem is by overprotecting them. Of course children need protection in many ways and are dependent upon us for various things at different stages of their lives. But we often extend this protection far beyond what our children actually need.

We often unintentionally overprotect children when they exhibit fear:

We divorced when my son was eight, and he suddenly became afraid of the dark. Every night it was a struggle for him to go to sleep. He'd cry and cry that "monsters" were in the dark and were going to get him. Every night, I was beside myself and ended up staying in his bed until he fell asleep. This went on for weeks. And then he'd wake up in the middle of the night, crying for me to come back or sleep in his room. I would go back and forth all night, trying to comfort him. I thought I was doing the right thing by telling him that I could see he was scared and I'd protect him. After about three months of this, I finally sought some professional help. A therapist pointed out that although my intentions were good and my son was going through an especially rough time, I was actually protecting him from something that wasn't real. By sleeping with him and telling him I'd protect him, I unintentionally validated his monster fantasy. The message he heard was, *Maybe there really are monsters*, because why else would Mom need to protect me?

This child didn't recognize that his mom was responding to his fear; he believed instead that she was responding to the monsters. For our children to feel capable and confident about their abilities, we must support their independence. This mother could have listened to her child's fears and acknowledged them by saying something like, "I know how sometimes things feel kind of scary, especially at night." She could have also provided supportive words that might have addressed the root of the problem—how difficult the divorce was for him.

She might also say, "This is a difficult time for you and for all of us. Sometimes when changes are happening, like Daddy and me getting divorced, things can feel a little unsafe and scary." She might then have reassured her son with words like, "It's safe here, and even though you feel scared sometimes, you can know that it's safe."

And finally, and perhaps most important, she could have encouraged his capabilities by saying, "I know you'll be able to fall asleep on your own. Can you think of anything we could do to help you feel braver? Would it help if we left the hall light on tonight?"

While it's okay to suggest things that might help her son feel less scared, the only one she shouldn't endorse is staying with him at night because of the monsters. If he suggests it, she might say, "I know you can do it on your own, and I wouldn't leave you anywhere that wasn't safe. Can you think of a way you can feel braver without Mommy staying?"

The conversation doesn't need to take too long (too long being more than thirty minutes or so). An appropriate ending, if no solution is reached, might be something like this: "You know, you're good at figuring things out, and I'm sure you'll be able to come up with an idea that will help. When you do, if you need my help for it, you let me know. I'll be right in the next room."

This kind of supportive, problem-solving approach empowers children by promoting their independence. Likewise, it builds their courage because while you're validating their feelings (in this case, fear), you're not validating the fictitious "monsters." Your child will be left with thoughts like, *Gee, it must be okay or Mom wouldn't have left. Also, she must trust that I can handle things myself. I guess I can!*

Of course, if the basis for the fear (or other emotion) is valid, for example if the child is saying, "I'm scared of you and Daddy getting a divorce," you'll want to acknowledge that both the fear and the divorce are real. You'll still, however, want to reassure your child by asking what might make him feel more comfortable.

With this approach it's also important to know what your child is capable of developmentally. While no child at any age needs to be slept with because she is afraid of monsters (because there are no real monsters), be sure that you provide appropriate support for your child's developmental level. For example, you don't want to empower your six-year old to tell his friends about the divorce if he feels afraid to do so. He may not know how or he may feel embarrassed or overwhelmed by that idea. It may add undue stress to expect that of him. In cases where your child isn't developmentally ready to assume a particular level of independence, you must step in and provide the support he needs.

To know if your child is ready, you need to not only take into account what you know about your child but also check out a book that addresses your child's age. Many times, children are far more capable than we give them credit for, and a book about development can provide an independent and objective point of view.

SHIFTING THE FOCUS

There are many times in life when we focus on the negative instead of the positive. Many people spend their lives choosing the "lesser of two evils" instead of the "better of two situations." It's the difference between looking at the glass as half-full or as half-empty. Sometimes parents look at their children, and their children's behavior, as half-empty instead of half-full.

When I was a kid, every night it was each child's job to rinse her dinner plate and put it in the dishwasher. Night after night, this was the routine, and night after night, I did it. My parents never said a word. One night toward the end of dinner, the phone rang and it was for me. Since I was almost finished, my mother allowed me to speak to my friend. I got so involved in the conversation that when I hung up the phone I completely forgot that my plate was still on the table. Well, my stepfather flew into a rage about my "irresponsible behavior." I remember thinking to myself that I must have done this the right way for hundreds of nights the and he never noticed. But the one time I do it wrong, I'm suddenly irresponsible. After that, I almost intentionally "forgot" to put the dish away and when I did "remember" I let him know how resentful I was.

This one incident had a lasting impact on this woman, because her stepfather failed to recognize when his stepchild was doing the right thing and, instead, pointed out her failings, which robbed her of self-esteem. In these cases, children are left with the feeling that "nothing is ever good enough. I'm never good enough. Why should I even try when trying results in nothing and only failing is noticed?"

Very soon, the child lives up to the "half-empty" expectations and begins to perform only halfway. If the stepfather had said, "Hon, I'd appreciate it if you'd put your dish away," and followed it the next night (when the stepdaughter did it without being asked) by saying, "You know, I noticed how you take responsibility for putting your dish away without being asked. I may not always mention it, but it doesn't go unnoticed," this woman would have carried a completely different feeling with her through life. She would have taken pride in being responsible and for doing things without being asked, rather than trying to find ways to "forget" her responsibility and feeling resentful when she was called on to be responsible. In addition, she would have felt closer to her stepfather, as well as supported by him.

To shift your focus, ask yourself these questions:

What has my child done right today?
What can I point out that I admired or was grateful for?
How has my child made me proud today?

Sometimes it takes a little practice to see the glass as half-full instead of half-empty, but once you begin to look for the positive in your child, it becomes a habit and ultimately helps you look at the bright side in other areas of your life as well.

BEING A ROLE MODEL

Another important aspect of empowering your child is being a role model. This is usually the part of empowerment that parents find most difficult, yet it's crucial. Most of us are conditioned (probably because of the way we were parented) to say things that diminish our own self-esteem or to discount positive feedback from others. We say things like, "I'm such a screwup," "I always blow it," "I never do anything right." In doing this, we not only begin a self-fulfilling process for ourselves, but we also model for our children that it's okay for them not to feel good about themselves, either.

Your child sees this attitude when someone attempts to bolster your self-esteem or courage with a caring thought like, "Wow, I really admire how you're coping," and in front of your child you respond with, "Really? I feel like a walking disaster area." Your child doesn't realize that this is an inappropriate, self-defeating response. She hears this and will likely react similarly when she is in a comparable situation.

In one of our workshops, we do an exercise where the participants give each other compliments. It's fascinating that many people find a way to negate the compliments they receive. One woman said, "I felt jealous of the compliments that were given to the other people. I wanted those compliments for myself." Yet the compliments paid to her were not only valid but also enviable: "sensitive," "open," "honest," "good sense of humor."

In order to show your children how to let in encouragement and allow it to work toward building their self-esteem, you, too, must acknowledge and accept comfort and support from others. By accepting compliments with "thank you" or "I appreciate your saying so," you show an acceptance of your strengths and help your children accept their strengths, too.

9.

When Your Ex Tops the Problem Pyramid

HOW TO COMMUNICATE WHEN THE PROBLEM BELONGS TO YOUR EX

As we've said before, when someone else has a problem we, very often willingly (though many times unknowingly), take on that problem as our own. We immediately begin thinking about ways to solve it, what we can do, and what we should say. And just as often, the person with the problem is more than happy to hand it right over and allow us to take it. After all, it relieves him or her of the burden of solving it. This is especially true in situations that involve your ex—in fact, not only would he prefer for you to solve his problems with regard to the children, many times he actually expects you to!

An additional complication lies in the fact that just because your ex tops the problem pyramid, it doesn't necessarily mean you're completely off the hook. While you might like to laugh and say, "That's your problem, you jerk! Figure it out for yourself," things are rarely that simple when your child is involved.

Your job, today and every day, is to be your child's advocate. As such you'll have to decide how to communicate with your ex about the problems he or she has in a way that benefits your child while not taking on the problem yourself. This can be tricky.

TAKING YOUR TIME

The first and perhaps most important lesson to learn is not to act too quickly when presented with a problem. When Jill answered the phone on Wednesday evening, she wasn't expecting a call from her ex, Mike. He began the conversation without preamble, saying, "Listen, Jill. I know it's my weekend to take Kristen and I'm really sorry, but I just got invited on a ski trip that I can't pass up, so you'll need to make other arrangements for her."

"Hold on a sec, Mike," she replied, "I'm in the middle of something. If you'll hang on two minutes I'll get right back to you. Or would you rather I hung up and called you back?"

"No, that's okay; I'll hold."

Jill made a smart move here. By putting Mike on hold, she gave herself a few minutes to think. Very often, when someone is trying to get us to take on their problem he or she relies heavily on the element of surprise.

Pressuring someone to act quickly is a highly manipulative maneuver. An ex who pressures you with deadlines is much like a salesperson who is hoping you'll make a purchase before doing some comparative shopping. Sometimes the pressure occurs at the beginning of the conversation, as with Mike and Jill; other times it occurs in the middle or even toward the end.

Whenever you begin to feel pressured, it's appropriate to say things like, "I'm glad I got to hear your side of it. Now I need to think it through and then make my decision." Or, "I know you want an answer right now, but it would be unfair to all of us if I didn't think this through. I'll get back to you in an hour." It's rarely in your best interest to act quickly, and it's usually to your advantage to wait. Don't be bullied into thinking you have to give an immediate answer or decision.

Jill's Reply

Jill gave herself a minute or two to reflect on what Mike had said, then got back on the phone.

"Thanks for waiting, Mike. Now, what were you saying?"

"I got invited by a client to go skiing this weekend. I need you to take Kristen."

"I see," Jill said. "Skiing sounds like fun."

"It's a good business opportunity as well."

"I'll bet! So what were your plans for Kristen?"

"What do you mean?" Mike seemed bewildered.

"What alternate arrangements did you have in mind for Kristen?"

"I want you to take her," said Mike in an exasperated tone. "We've talked about this, Jill, and we agreed that it's better for her to be with a parent than a babysitter. And you *are* her other parent, after all," he added sarcastically.

"You're right, I am," said Jill. "I have plans myself this

weekend, so I can't help you out this time. What else do you think might work?"

"Nothing, Jill! I don't want her with a babysitter."

"I understand that. In that case, it sounds like you might have to reschedule your ski trip. If you decide you want to hire a babysitter, though, it's okay with me. Here's the number of one we've used before." Jill recited the number over the phone.

"All right, I'll deal with it," Mike replied with disgust. "God, you're impossible."

Jill handled this situation beautifully. She recognized that Mike was trying to hand his problem over to her, and she refused to accept it.

RECOGNIZING BULLYING TECHNIQUES

The first thing Jill did that contributed to her success was recognize the techniques that Mike was using to bully her into taking on his problem. Let's take a look at these techniques.

Communicating Assumptions

Assumptions are a leveraging technique that many people use to avoid solving their own problems. Mike leads with an assumption by saying, "I need you to take Kristen." The implication is that Jill doesn't have plans herself for the weekend or that she will readily change plans to accommodate him.

Referencing a Prior Agreement

When Jill doesn't immediately take on Mike's child-care problem, he attempts to convince her that this is something upon which they've already agreed: "We've talked about this, Jill, and we agreed that it's better for her to be with a parent than a babysitter." Referencing a general agreement in a specific situation is a bullying tactic. While it's true that Jill agreed that *ideally* it's better for Kristen to be taken care of by a parent, abstract agreements are not meant to be ironclad. There will always be exceptions that arise that must be considered on a case-by-case basis.

Using Sarcasm

Mike says, "You *are* her other parent, after all." Sarcastic communication is designed to make the recipient feel foolish and embarrass him or her into changing his or her mind.

Refusal to Negotiate

When Jill attempts to brainstorm by saying, "What else do you think might work?" Mike tries cutting her off by saying, "Nothing, Jill! I don't want her with a babysitter." Remember what we said previously about the words "always" and "never"? The word "nothing" falls into this same category. There are many things that could work in this situation, but by saying that "nothing" will work Mike is trying to strong-arm Jill into accepting responsibility for the problem.

REMAINING NON-DEFENSIVE

By recognizing the bullying techniques that Mike uses, Jill is able to successfully avoid taking on this problem. Let's now look at the specific techniques she uses to remain engaged in productive communication.

Jill does a good job remaining non-defensive in her conversation with Mike. Negotiations between ex-spouses are often stalled before they get started because one or both parties come to the table with angry words and behaviors. When that happens, the other partner, even if he wasn't angry in the first place, can become defensive and respond to the other's angry tone and actions with anger of his own. Once both people are acting in an angry manner, a stalemate often results. Both parties end the conversation and go back to their children to regale them with tales of what a jerk their father or mother is.

Non-defensive responses help your ex feel as though you're listening to his side of the situation. This is important because when someone feels understood he's less likely to escalate with words, tone, or body language to get his point of view across. Escalation happens when the person's thought processes go something like this: *She must not understand how I feel and what I want. If she really understood the situation, she wouldn't refuse.*

Non-defensive statements make it clear that you understand. Here are a few to get you started:

That's an interesting way to see it.

So what you're saying is that . . .

That's difficult.

I see.

I hear you.

Gee, that does sound like a problem.

What a dilemma you must be in!

I know how hard it can be to turn down a trip because of the kids.

Sometimes, despite your best efforts at communicating that you understand what your ex is saying, he or she will belabor the point. If this occurs, it's helpful to say something along the lines of, "What would help you know that I understand what you're saying?" or, "What would you like to hear from me?" If at any point your ex responds with, "Why are you talking like this?" or, "Quit pretending you're a shrink," you may be sounding too stilted and it's time to ease up. Go back to, "Uh-huh," "mmmm," and other non-verbal but vocal listening cues.

HANDING THE PROBLEM BACK

Before you hand the problem back to your ex, you need to be convinced of your own boundaries or limits. Jill had other plans for her weekend, and that was a limit she wasn't willing to negotiate. She let Mike know this when she said, "I have plans myself this weekend, so I can't help you out this time." She then turned the problem-solving process back to Mike by saying, "What else do you think might work?"

We support another person in solving his or her own problems when we ask questions like these:

How are you going to handle that?

I wonder what would happen if you . . . [rescheduled the ski weekend for a time when you don't have child-care responsibilities, brought Kristen with you, took her to your sister's house]?"

I understand. Can you think of any way to handle the situation with Kristen?

Make no mistake, it will probably take a lot of courage to say these things, especially if you're not used to being assertive. It's difficult to hand a problem back to its rightful owner, especially if the owner is not convinced that it belongs to him in the first place!

It's also important to understand that if Jill had no plans and *was* willing to take their daughter for the weekend, then this was not a battle she should pick just for the sake of making Mike solve his own problems. If she didn't have plans but still wanted to communicate that it was his problem, she could have said, "Luckily, I don't have plans this weekend, so I'm happy to help you out."

AGREEING WITH CONTENT

Another technique Jill uses successfully occurs when Mike attempts to bait Jill by using sarcasm. Rather than responding to his sarcastic tone of voice, she avoids the confrontation by agreeing with the *content* of Mike's communication, saying, "You're right; I am [her other parent]." She continues by presenting the fact that she, too, has plans and initiates brainstorming by saying, "What else do you think might work?"

Let's take a look at another problem owned by an ex and see how Cheryl handles it. You'll notice that we put the communication techniques in parentheses.

Piano Problems

My ex really wants our daughter to learn to play piano and I couldn't care less. He's always calling me to see if she's practicing and it's making me nuts!

After discerning that her ex tops the problem pyramid, Cheryl decides to prepare herself for the next phone call. Sure enough, only hours after her ex drops their daughter off he calls.

"Cheryl, we have to talk." (Using the element of surprise)

"What's up, Bill?"

"You know what's up—Diana had her piano lesson today

and she sounded terrible. I can't believe she practiced at all when she was at your house last week. You absolutely have to set up practice times with her." (Trying to get Cheryl to take problem)

"She didn't do well during her lesson." (Listening)

"Damn right she didn't. How could she? You never make her practice." (Assumption)

"I know how much you care about her practicing. Can you think of a way to approach her about it?"(Non-defensive response plus brainstorming)

"Cheryl! I just asked you to make her practice. It's not going to kill you to be a mother for a change and make her practice." (Refusal to negotiate plus sarcasm combined with a derogatory accusation)

"I know you'd like me to make her practice, Bill. I hear that the lessons are very important to you. I think it would mean something coming from you if you were to speak with her about it yourself." (Listening plus positive assertion)

"There you go again, avoiding your responsibility." (Insult)

"I have to run now. I'm sure that when you speak with her she'll respond well." (Assumption)

Cheryl does a good job not taking the bait here, staying focused and refusing to take on Bill's problem with their daughter. Her own assumption at the end ("I'm sure that when you speak with her she'll respond well") serves as a positive expectation.

Cheryl also could have been more direct about her positive assertion, saying, "I hear how important the piano is to you.

I'd like for you to talk to Diana about it. I'm choosing battles here and this is one that I'm not interested in choosing."

CLICK! THE EX WHO AVOIDS

I knew my ex ran from problems, but it really became evident after we separated. We were arguing a lot over money, visitation, parenting, all the usual things, and she started to hang up on me. I'd be right in the middle of telling her why I thought she should or should not do something and I'd hear *click!* It was so annoying that I would call her back and shout obscenities and then hang up on her.

Sometimes your ex is so intent on avoiding her problems that she simply hangs up on you in the middle of the conversation. Banging down telephones, slamming doors, not answering texts or email messages, and especially, uncontrolled raging effectively cut off communication between you and your ex, and your ex knows it. When your ex engages in one of these behaviors, your first reaction may be to retaliate. You may be so angry that you want to text or pick up the phone and scream, "You jerk, how dare you . . . !" However, this is not the most effective way to handle avoiders. Instead, try holding back your response and redirecting your reaction. You might try calling a friend to vent or using the vacuum that's produced by an avoidant ex as an opportunity to plan a strategy for being heard.

What happens, though, when your ex is so stubborn about not looking at the problem that every strategy you try isn't working? If that's the case, you may need to claim the top of the pyramid yourself.

CLAIMING THE TOP OF THE PYRAMID

When your ex does cut off communication (abruptly or otherwise), it may be necessary to deal with the issue as your problem, regardless of who originally topped the problem pyramid. "Not fair," you say. And you're right. But remember that the goal here is to keep your children out of your conflicts so they're not hurt in the divorce process. If that means you need to formulate an "I" statement and a positive assertion and call your ex back, do it. If it means that you need to engage the help of a professional, then do that. It will give you good experience for the future.

NEEDING LEGAL OR PROFESSIONAL HELP

If your ex continually abdicates his or her visitation responsibilities, regularly harasses you, constantly mistreats your child, or frequently misses child support payments, you may need to seek professional help. Notice that we use the words "continually," "regularly," "constantly," and "frequently." Occasional behaviors may go away by themselves. But when occasional behaviors become commonplace, stricter measures must be employed. If you need a therapist, find one. If you need a lawyer (or a better lawyer than you have), get one. If you need the police, call them, now! If it's your ex who needs the therapist, you can suggest seeing one together, but don't get your hopes up. Sometimes the most you can do is send your ex a copy of this book and hope he or she reads it.

Finding a Counselor or Therapist

If you really believe that your ex needs help, you might suggest joint counseling for "parenting issues." But if your goal is to get your ex into therapy for his or her own good, give up. The only person you can change is you. Finding a therapist or counselor for yourself will help you deal more effectively with the feelings that come up in connection with your ex.

For some people, the thought of seeing a therapist or counselor evokes shame, but in reality therapy and counseling are more like taking a course in "self." Think of therapy as a map to life. Most of us eventually find our way, but looking at a map or asking for directions makes the process much easier.

Other people hesitate to call a therapist or counselor because they feel that seeing one means they'll have to go for the rest of their life. The truth is that if you like the process (and the results), you can make it a long-term relationship. But if you prefer to set a time frame, most therapists or counselors are willing to work within it. Say, "I'm having a hard time with my ex right now and I'd like to spend three months [or six or twelve months] exploring what I can do to make this process easier."

If the counselor or therapist you speak to doesn't like time frames, you can find someone else. It's also important to make sure that the therapist or counselor you choose is specifically trained in divorce and stepfamily dynamics and in communication skills.

Whether you decide to go into counseling is up to you. We do recommend, however, that you seek professional help immediately if you notice that your child is suffering. This may mean therapy for your child, for you, or for both of you.

Signs that your child needs professional help include poor school performance when it was good before, unusually aggressive or lethargic behavior, excessive weight gain or loss, mood swings that range from extreme hostility to overt affection, and uncharacteristic and intense tantrums and overreactions. Negative changes in your child's behavior, such as lying, cheating, stealing, and drug or alcohol use, are also signs that your child is having a hard time.

How each of your children handles the divorce may differ. A child's birth order, personality, age, and gender can all play a part in how resilient he or she is. Someone once likened divorce to being in a car accident. How it affects you depends, in part, on where you were sitting. That being said, most of the time kids are flexible and can survive divorce, along with most other family crises, as long as they have a supportive home environment, a sense of structure in their lives, and genuine love and caring from at least one parent.

WHEN YOUR EX'S "OTHER" TOPS THE PROBLEM PYRAMID

The Case of the Wimpy Stepfather

If your ex has formed a new relationship, you may find there will be times when a problem seems to belong to your ex when, in fact, he is actually acting under pressure from his current spouse or significant other. Consider Sam's story:

> Whenever our son gets even a minor illness, my ex starts rearranging the visitation plans. It's as if she doesn't want him to spend the night or have contact with her new husband, but she still wants to see him. So she'll call me sounding desperate and ask if she can just take him for the day, to the zoo or to the park, and return him before dinner. Or she'll ask if she can take him for a few hours to a movie instead of overnight. I really think her new husband is behind this. He's got a high-powered job and seems absolutely paranoid about getting sick and missing work. I want my ex to see our son, and she does, too, but one time she even wanted me to rearrange visitation because I mentioned that our son had athlete's foot.

This type of problem is the most difficult to sort out because it has a snowball effect, where one person passes a problem to another, who takes it on and passes it to you. It's often difficult to see where the problem originates and which parties need to handle it.

Obviously, we can't be a bug on the wall and know exactly what's happening in Sam's ex-wife's house. However, that shouldn't deter Sam from handling this with his ex. Here's how the problem pyramid breaks down, using Sam's suspicions as well as the facts as a guide:

Who has the upset feelings?

New husband.

Who brought up the issue?

New husband (tells wife he doesn't want her child around because he might get sick).

Who is responsible for implementing the solution?

New husband.

Because Sam has no contact with the new husband of his ex, the problem needs to be looked at from a different angle, so here's what really matters: The wife has a problem because she wants to see her son, but she also wants to accommodate her new husband. Rather than standing her ground with him, she comes to Sam and it breaks down this way:

Who has the upset feelings?

Sam's ex.

Who brought up the issue?

Sam's ex.

Who is responsible for implementing the solution?

Sam's ex.

Let's see how Sam refrains from taking on the problem that exists between his ex and her new husband:

"Sam, it's Robin. How's Danny doing?"

"Fine. He's had a little sniffle recently, but he seems to be getting over it."

"A sniffle?! Do you think it's contagious?"

"You sound concerned," Sam replied, using his empathy techniques.

"Well, no," Robin hedged. "I mean . . . well, anyway, um, I guess I was wondering if I could just have Danny during the day Saturday. I'd like to take him to the zoo, but something's come up for Saturday night and so I don't think I can have him over for the night."

"Is there something I can help with, Robin? I hear a little hedging in your voice. Is there a problem with Danny being sick that I don't know about?"

Sometimes an attitude of sympathy can help you get to the bottom of a problem. In first asking if he can help, then reflecting the feeling he heard in Robin's voice, Sam is more likely to get to the root of the problem.

Robin replied, "Uh, no. I mean, well, it's just that Mark has an important project coming up and he can't afford to get sick.

So I thought I'd just take Danny to the zoo so Mark wouldn't catch whatever he might have."

"Oh, I see," said Sam. "It sounds like Mark is concerned about getting sick and missing work and that's why you haven't been taking Danny when he's not one hundred percent. Is that right?" (Here Sam simply restated the facts, then checked in with, "Is that right?")

"Well, yeah," Robin admitted. "I just feel kind of stuck, because I really want to see Danny."

"I guess you *must* feel kind of stuck. After all, kids always have some kind of minor ailment, and Danny's been no exception this past winter. Sounds like it's hard on you to be missing out on so much visitation. I guess you discussed with Mark the fact that Danny isn't always contagious."

"Well, sort of."

"I wonder what would happen if you pointed that out to him? If his only objection about Danny spending the night is when Danny's contagious, maybe he'll be willing to have him overnight if he knows he's not. Or maybe it would be easier for you if I didn't tell you about every minor thing Danny's had recently."

"Maybe."

"This sounds like a difficult issue for you, Robin. Why don't I go ahead and plan on not mentioning Danny's health unless he's contagious? That way you don't get caught in that bind."

"Well, okay, I guess. But what about Saturday?"

"It happens that I can keep Danny on this particular Saturday night, although I'd like you to tell him yourself, so if he's disappointed you can handle it."

"Okay, and thanks, Sam."

Sam did a good job here of handling the problem. Although it still may appear that he took it on (because he's keeping Danny on Saturday night), he made what might possibly be great inroads for the future. Finding out what Robin's real issue is (rather than just assuming) enables Sam to simply not mention Danny's health to her unless it's serious. Meanwhile, Sam's made the subtle suggestion that if Robin could communicate directly with Mark, it might be beneficial to everyone concerned. In addition, Sam's made it plain that Robin will have to handle their son's potential disappointment herself, which might ultimately serve as a motivator for her to stand up to her husband, Mark.

This conversation represents an awful lot of work for Sam (though not as much work as having a screaming fight with Robin), but he's clearly kept his number-one priority in mind— Danny. It's in Danny's best interests for Sam to spend extra time and effort to encourage his ex to look at solutions to this problem. While it may seem as though he's almost serving in the capacity of therapist (which is not appropriate, by the way), the communication remained short.

Had things dragged on and on, had Robin been unwilling to look at solutions or admit there was a problem, Sam simply could have stood firm about his boundaries and left Robin to figure out for herself how to handle a sick child with her new husband. For example, Sam might have said, "I can see your problem, Robin. It sounds as if Mark is very worried about catching something. But I have made other plans and Danny is not that sick." That's definitely the shorter route, but sometimes it's in the child's best interests, especially when the problem is recurring, to take a little extra time, probe a little deeper, and try cooperatively to arrive at a solution.

THE ROLE OF THE STEPPARENT

This is not primarily a book about stepparenting, but it is appropriate to say a word about the role that stepparents can play when they're married to someone who can be a jerk with joint-custody issues.

Being a stepparent is a difficult and often unrewarding job. Think of all the fairy tales where the stepparent gets a bad rap and you have a not too unrealistic picture of society's view of stepparents. Yet in the majority of cases the bad press that stepparents get is unjustified. Stepparents can provide a loving, supportive, understanding presence that enriches a child's life immeasurably.

If you delve beneath the surface of those fairy tales, you can see the difficulties that stepparents face. The doting biological parent ignores the misbehavior of the children, creating more work for the stepparent, who feels left out, resentful, and angry at the "raw deal" she or he was dealt. After all, the stepparent fell in love with another adult, not with the stepchildren, yet they always seem to be around, interfering with the marriage. Likewise, the biological parent isn't always approachable about the subject.

In cases where the parent has joint custody with a jerk, the issues are even more complicated for the stepparent. Not only does he or she have to deal with the children, he or she has to deal with the ex (in absentia) as well. While the ex may not be physically present, the ex who is a jerk makes his presence known as he or she lives on (psychologically) in the daily life of the parent and of the children. A stepparent is then dealing not only with the reality of someone else's children but also with his or her spouse's frustration, anger, helplessness, and complaints about the ex. Many times it feels as if the ex is actually living with the new couple. In addition, the mistakes that ex has made with the children take their toll because the children very often act out, misbehave, and have a lack of consideration for the rules in the stepparent's home. Consider the following:

My husband's son, James, who is seven, came to visit us. We have two children of our own, five and three years old. Well, the first few days were okay, until my husband went to work and I had all three kids. James picked up a stick in the park and was swinging it around. I asked him to please stop, because I was afraid he might hit the other kids, and he said, "Good! I'll hit 'em all. My mom hits me; why can't I hit them?"

Well, I was shocked. My husband and I don't believe in hitting our children. So later I asked James to tell me what he meant, and he shrugged and said, "My mom has to hit me 'cause I'm a bad boy." I said, "James, it must hurt your feelings when that happens." Well, it was like I'd opened a

Pandora's box. He began to sob and all this stuff came pouring out. He said, "I'm bad. Mommy hits me when I'm bad, but there's no one there to protect me. You're not supposed to hit people, but Mommy hits me when I'm bad. I have to go," and he started to walk away from me. I said, "James, let's talk about it," and he said, "No, my mommy doesn't let me be around people when I'm upset because I'm a bad boy."

I have to tell you I didn't know what to do with all this stuff this poor kid was suffering with. I tried my best to just be sympathetic, but it was too difficult to get through. The rest of the day was awful. James had a lot of anger and it just came pouring out. By the end of the day, my kids were a wreck and so was I. And truthfully, I began to lose some of my sympathy when it started affecting my kids. I mean, who was this woman who had so much power over all our lives?

This kind of scenario is not unusual. Very often, the stepparent is placed in a position of being a confidante to the child and, as in this case, in the awkward position of protecting her own children from the stepchild. What the stepmother did next, however, shows insight and skill in handling the situation with her husband:

When my husband got home, I decided to let him have some downtime instead of coming right at him with my concerns. I'm so glad I did! Between the time he got home and the time the kids went to bed, he had already experienced some of what I had during the day. All three kids were clingy and needy, verbally as well as physically, and picking on one another.

It was so unusual for our kids to be that way that my husband asked me what was going on. I suggested that we wait until the kids were in bed to talk and he agreed. When we sat down later, I told him that it looked like he was concerned (instead of focusing on myself), and he brought up the children's behavior. Rather than get defensive about our kids being included with his (since I saw James as the perpetrator), I simply relayed what James had told me earlier about being hit.

Well, my husband was equally shocked—and furious at his ex as well! It provided a really good entry to a discussion that might not have been possible if I had exploded about the tough day I'd had. It was worth keeping my feelings to myself for just a little while, because my husband was much more open to hearing them after I told him about James in a sympathetic way.

When your spouse's children are with you, schedule routine talks with your spouse. And let him or her air feelings first. Whenever possible, try to be empathetic about your stepchild's behavior, recognizing that often the behavior is a result of the ex:

I have to say, our discussion went on for a long time, and I tried hard to see my husband's point of view, because he did feel defensive at times during our conversation. I tried to focus on his feelings, and truthfully, he was equally concerned about the impact that James was having on our kids. I told him what I wanted, too—that his ex needed to be approached about her parenting because it was so obviously affecting James. I tried to keep our kids out of it, even though it was hard. I could see that my husband was feeling a little overwhelmed, so I also gave him a concrete suggestion about how to approach her.

When possible, avoid simply airing your feelings without having a plan of action to suggest. In all likelihood, your spouse is also feeling overwhelmed and needs specific suggestions for what to do.

It can be very rewarding to act as a team. Don't make it "our kids" versus "your kids" or your spouse will become protective and close off communication. Call a professional for help if you get stuck.

The primary role of a stepparent is to be part of the solution, not part of the problem. Read chapter 7, "When Your Child Tops the Problem Pyramid," for supportive techniques that won't put your spouse on the defensive. These techniques are appropriate to use with your children, stepchildren, or others as well. Remember that you can take your feelings to a friend or counselor, but the most effective way to get through to your spouse is through teamwork, not a "me versus you" mentality.

10.

Communicating in Our Digital World

CAN YOU HEAR ME NOW?

If you had to pick one word or phrase to exemplify how the world has changed in the past twenty years, it might be "computers." A runner-up might be "cell phones," which in many cases are computers as well.

Twenty years ago, when you needed to talk to your ex you had to call him or her on the phone or meet face-to-face. Many of the minute details of parenting were lost because parents couldn't get in touch with each other immediately. Sometimes the lack of immediacy caused frustration or anger, but sometimes it was a relief not to have to cooperate on every little thing.

Today, nearly everyone has a cell phone, which allows for instant connectivity. In fact, this digital force seems omnipresent and has even changed the language we use to communicate. "B there in 20," "Did you 'friend' him?" and "C U soon" are messages understood by almost everyone. This new method of communication can have its advantages:

Computers?! Heck, I remember, years ago, how thrilled I was when our office got a fax machine because that meant I could fax notes and bills and papers to my ex and I didn't have to hear her stupid voice. And then there was that Christmas morning when our daughter was really little and I waited an hour at the wrong gas station to hand her off to my ex. Or that time I got lost taking her to her grandmother's house. Now I have a new ex, and luckily, between my cell phone and GPS, I don't have these problems anymore. I'm so glad times have changed.

Indeed, times and methods of communication have progressed so much that we thought it warranted this chapter—to explore today's technology and how it can impact your divorce. Our goal is to help you protect yourself from misunderstanding through miscommunication, to prevent you from unintentionally revealing any personal information, and to take advantage of the benefits our digital world presents.

COMMUNICATING DIGITALLY

In chapter 4 we mentioned the work of Dr. Albert Mehrabian, Professor Emeritus of Psychology at UCLA. In his research, he discovered that communication is essentially made up of three components: words, tone of voice, and body language. He states that 7 percent of our feelings or attitudes are communicated via our words, 38 percent by our tone of voice, and 55 percent by our body language (the 7-38-55 percent rule). If our words are incongruent with either our body language or our tone of voice, the listener is likely to interpret what we're saying based on the non-verbal cues rather than the words themselves. For example, words that alone may sound neutral such as "He's your father" take on a completely different meaning when said with a sarcastic tone, "He's *your* father," and an eye roll. Conversely, words that may sound harsh if viewed alone may be softened by body language or tone or both. For example, "You're not going to be on time" might initially appear to be a criticism. However, with a head shake and a wry smile it could be construed as teasing in a loving way.

In digital communication such as emailing, texting, tweeting, or posting, the lack of non-verbal cues can lead to a misinterpretation of the words the sender is using. While emoticons (i.e., ☺, ;-), :P, and the like) are a way that we've attempted to insert a form of body language into our typed messages, they're a poor substitute for the body language we see when speaking face-to-face or for the tone in a voice-to-voice conversation.

When deciding what form of communication you should use to address your ex, it's helpful to keep the 7-38-55 percent rule in mind. Ask yourself, *Would what I'm about to communicate be helped or hurt by my tone of voice? Would my body language or facial expression soften this communication or would I be unable to control either? By themselves, can these words be misconstrued?* If you have trouble deciding, consult a friend—especially when you choose to type rather than call or meet with your ex.

TEXTING TEMPTATION

Texts (as well as instant messages) are an informal means of communication and thus are great for letting the other person know a short bit of information quickly. They are, however, almost never appropriate for important conversations, major discussions, and, especially, bad news.

Because texts are informal and quick, it can be tempting to use them as your main means of communication with your ex. But let's hear how one parent feels when her ex texts her about a sudden change in plans:

> I'm so angry I could scream! My ex was supposed to meet us at school for our son's play and he just sent me a text message saying: "Sorry can't make it."

Sending important messages via text is the coward's way out. In all likelihood, this woman's ex-husband knew that if he had called and spoken to her, he'd have had to engage in a longer conversation as well as face her disappointment. Texting effectively allowed him to avoid her and left the problem of telling their son in her hands.

So the first lesson here is don't be the person who texts important messages. It's rude, inconsiderate, and, yes, cowardly. The second lesson has to do with what you can do if you're on the receiving end of a text like this one.

This is where body language comes in—yours! Regardless of how angry you are, do not throw the phone. You will regret that later. The best thing to do in a situation like this is wait until you have processed your feelings and done what needs to get done before you respond. If your ex can't make it, he or she can wait to hear how upset you are and how disappointed your child will be until after you've calmed down and told your child.

Now, tone of voice—again yours. You need to calm down before you tell your child that Mom or Dad is not coming. You don't want to upset your child before his big moment. Try to step away from your anger and the disappointment you feel for your child and throw yourself into the pleasure of the activity your child is engaged in. Remember, too, that sometimes receiving a text message can be a blessing. From it you know your ex is not coming, and while you don't know why, at least you didn't have to listen to any of his or her sorry or lame excuses on the phone.

Texting is not all bad, of course. You've probably mastered the best use of texting for yourself and know that texts are efficient for quick and impersonal messages like: "Will pik up Timmy @ 2." We don't want to get locked into any strict "dos and don'ts," but here are a few general tips to use texting technology to your advantage.

Keep It Simple

- If you find yourself going back and forth via text, consider picking up the phone instead. Texting is great if it involves short bullet point-type messages, but the more back-and-forth there is, the greater the chance for miscommunication.

- Be clear. Sometimes, in a word-saving effort people become so cryptic that needless misunderstandings occur.
- Unless you're absolutely positive that your text has been received, don't assume that it was. Remember what we've said about making assumptions in previous chapters.
- If you get a text (or for that matter a phone call or email) from your ex while you are driving, ignore it until you arrive at your destination.
- Your phone has an off button. You are allowed to use it in places other than at the movies.
- Don't feel that you have to reply to a text immediately. More often than not, taking extra time will yield greater benefits.
- Don't drink and dial, text, email, IM, or post to Facebook.
- Remember that a text (like an IM or email) can be printed, kept, forwarded, and potentially used in court.
- You can't really be sure who is at the other end of the text. Even though the phone or computer belongs to your ex, he or she can hand it to a friend or co-worker to read and answer.

I SEE YOU

Instant messages (IMs) and iChats are useful and fun. If you are my buddy, I may see you on my buddy list, say hi, chat for a few minutes, and go on with my day. But if you are my ex and we are on each other's buddy lists, I may see you and you may see me when we don't want to see each other:

> I feel like my ex is stalking me online. He leaves me voice mails that say: "I see you logged off at 3:08 p.m. Weren't you supposed to pick Joel up at 3:00 from soccer practice?"

Buddy lists open a window for "cyberstalking," and keeping track of your ex's whereabouts (or inadvertently allowing him or her to keep an eye on where you are) throughout the day based upon whether you see him or her logged on.

Except in extremely congenial divorces, we believe that taking your ex off your buddy or instant chat list, adopting a new and private screen name, or blocking your ex from your list is an important boundary to set. If necessary, you may also want to change your email and log on with your friends under your new screen name. There is no reason for your ex to know exactly when you are online.

If you do choose to communicate online with your ex, remember to keep your interactions polite and thoughtful. If you wouldn't want what you're saying put up on a billboard for the entire world to see, then you shouldn't be writing it to your ex. A simple message could be viewed and answered by a coworker, your ex's new lover, or your child.

> I was IMing my ex about an electric bill he hadn't paid, and I was being a little dramatic, saying that *he* would have to

explain to Kelly why she couldn't watch TV when they shut off our electricity. I guess he left the IM open and walked away from his computer and a few minutes later Kelly went to see if I was online and she read the IM. Then she called me, crying that she didn't want us to lose our electricity and telling me that I had to "make" Daddy pay the bill today.

EMAIL EQUALS

Email has revolutionized the way we communicate. What once took hours to write and days to arrive now takes minutes to type and nanoseconds to arrive. Or sometimes, if we're angry, seconds to type and send.

There's no question that putting your thoughts on paper is a great way to relieve stress, figure out what you're really thinking and feeling, and get something off your chest. But the best course is to leave the "To:" field blank when you're writing so you don't accidently press "send" before you're ready. Furthermore, after composing an email, send it to yourself or save it as a draft and then sleep on it, reread it, edit it, and sometimes abandon it. You may have realized, while using some of the techniques in this book, that your ex really doesn't care how you feel or what you think anymore. So write those e-letters and send them to yourself. Someday, you may have all the components for a best-selling book filed away in your in-box!

You may also receive an email that drives you to dash off a response as quickly as you can hit send. When you get an email like this, take a deep breath and remember that there's no law that says you have to answer immediately. Walk away from your computer, BlackBerry, or iPhone and get a drink of water. In fact, a good rule of thumb is to drink five glasses of water because (1) it's healthy and (2) it keeps your hands and mouth busy so you don't say or do something you might regret! When you are ready to craft your reply, remember, before you punch that send button, that this email can live forever.

A long and important email is the modern equivalent to a long and important letter, so use it in the same way. Take your time to write your emails, put some thought into them, state your case eloquently, but don't expect the recipient to realize how much time, thought, and eloquence you put into it. In fact, always remember that the recipient can "delete" your email upon arrival without reading it or give it only a cursory glance and go on.

> I once spent days, literally a whole weekend, composing a long email to my ex, telling him how I felt and what I thought we should do. I went back and forth, carefully choosing each word and weighing each thought. And then I sent it and got a response back, not ten seconds later, that said: "Okay." It was totally unsatisfying, especially in light of the time I put into my email.

In addition, an email you receive may not necessarily come from the person you think it's from:

> I hadn't been in touch with my ex for a while because our daughter was older, but I wrote to him to tell him that my

JOINT CUSTODY WITH A JERK

uncle had passed away. He wrote back a long email with perfect spelling and punctuation, which was odd, because he always typed without the right punctuation and couldn't spell at all. Then I realized that his new wife had answered my email. It was really creepy.

Email should be used judiciously, always remembering the 7-38-55 percent rule. If you feel that your email (or response to your ex's email) could be misinterpreted without tone of voice or body language or both to accompany it, don't send it. Make a call or schedule an appointment with your ex instead.

HE'S GOT MAIL

No matter what, don't read your ex's email. It's not only dishonest, which it is, and sneaky, which it is, and low, which it is, but you may also come away with information you shouldn't or don't want to have. To protect yourself, change your passwords so your ex can't access your accounts. Maybe it's time, too, for a whole new email address to acknowledge your whole new life! The added benefit is that you know you will never have a message waiting for you from your ex in your new in-box.

FACE IT

Social networking sites such as Facebook, YouTube, and Twitter are an entertaining, excellent, and easy way to keep in touch with friends and family. But by logging into these or similar sites and posting photos, status updates, links, and videos, you are opening up yourself to the public and to your ex:

> I couldn't believe it. I posted photos of our son's fourth birthday party on Facebook. The kids looked so cute sitting around the living room at their little tables with their paper hats on. Well, my ex saw the photos and went nuts. I didn't realize it, but in the background you can see the new flat-screen TV I just got. My parents bought it for me, but my ex is now talking about taking me back to court, claiming that I'm spending the child support money on foolish things.

> Then my older daughter, who is sixteen, posted a photo on Facebook of herself and her friends with beer cans in their hands. It's not that they were actually drinking. All the kids were doing this exact same thing at the time. But my ex called Child Services and reported me for serving alcohol to a minor. It was a mess.

If you really want to share photos with your friends and family, consider posting them to a photo site that is accessed by invitation. Shutterfly, Flickr, Zoomr, and KODAK Gallery are a few of the sites that allow you to share photos privately. Remember that once you post something to Facebook or You-Tube, it can be on the Internet forever:

> My ex is all over Facebook with his new woman. And then he posts photos of our kids on his site. He's still friends with

a lot of my friends, and even though we are not connected as friends, I see the photos of that woman swimming with my kids in Jamaica while I'm here in cold New Jersey and I get crazy.

If seeing photos of your ex's new woman in Jamaica is hard for you to handle, you may need to put up some boundaries to protect yourself. For instance, you may need to "unfriend" the people you know who will lead you right to your ex's wall. Obviously, you can "request," either in person or via an email, that your ex keeps the children off of Facebook for now, but don't count on it. You may be much happier if you just walk away from Facebook for a few months. Then do something positive for yourself, like meet some new friends, attend a book club, take up a hobby, or join an exercise class that has a social element to it. Or maybe even start planning your own trip, even if you can't take a vacation right now.

A COMMUNICATION DISASTER

I was turning forty around the same time our son was turning five. I planned a party for him and a party for myself on the same weekend. On the morning of his party, I was all set for that but hadn't really started getting ready for my party. In a moment of feeling forty and old, I wrote on Twitter: "It's party time and I'm so not ready for this birthday!" The next thing I know, my ex is on the phone, screaming at me that if I can't handle a simple birthday party, I shouldn't have planned it, and that his mother is on her way over with a cake, and why didn't I just bake one, which would have been cheaper. Then his sister called and we pieced together that his mother had seen my tweet and told her, "Ben's party is falling through the cracks. You know Anna works too much and probably forgot to get a cake! I'm going to pick one up and take it over."

Like many of the examples in this book, there is more than one miscommunication going on here. Anna started it with a tweet that was totally misinterpreted by her ex-mother-in-law, who then misreported it to her son, who then jumped to his own conclusions. While there's no cure for Anna's ex-mother-in-law's or her ex's behavior, this is another example of how an innocent statement on Twitter or Facebook can get in the wrong hands and take off in the wrong direction.

If you are going through a difficult divorce, draw your curtains occasionally so the world can't see you. Then regroup within your own circle. We're not suggesting social isolation, just discretion on the part of your personal network.

PLAY IT AGAIN, SAM

Remember the voice mail heard round the world? Well, we're not referring to any one specifically but to all of them in general. While it's certainly frustrating to be furious and find your ex not at the other end of the phone, the worst thing you can do is leave an angry voice mail that's any longer than: "Hi, I'm really angry right now. Call me back." Any message that starts: "How dare you . . ." or "I can't believe you . . ." is going to come back and bite you. And if, at this point, you're still thinking of leaving a message like this, please go back and reread chapter 2.

I JUST CALLED TO SAY I DON'T LOVE YOU

If you take a minute to look around you at the mall, on the street, or in your car, nearly everyone is on the cell phone. While some people are laughing and some are just making plans, you have probably heard someone having a loud and full-blown fight on a cell. When this happens on a bus or train or just walking down the street, it's ugly.

If your ex calls and you feel the conversation is rising to a dramatic level, politely say that you're on a cell phone in a public place and find out when you can call your ex back. If it's an urgent issue, find a quiet place to have your conversation.

NO HYPE WITH SKYPE

We've spent the majority of this chapter talking about the pitfalls of technology in the divorced home. Sometimes, though, technology can be helpful rather than hurtful:

Skype has been a terrific thing for us. Our kids are three and five and my ex travels for weeks and sometimes months at a time. It's really hard for the kids to engage with him on the phone. While Skype doesn't take the place of a visit, at least the kids can "see" Daddy and hold up their artwork, show him their new toys, and things like that.

Obviously, Skype can be problematic in the same way that Facebook photos can—for example, your ex might see something in the background that provokes an angry response. That being said, it does follow the 7-38-55 percent rule, allowing for "complete communication."

PICK A DATE

Many people are using Internet-based calendars to make sure that everyone—parents and kids—know their schedules. OurFamilyWizard.com, which carries an annual charge per parent, is set up for divorced parents and has a lot of excellent features. A free option is Google Calendar, which can easily be adapted for your needs. Set up a new account with your ex-spouse and post upcoming events such as birthday parties, piano recitals, and volleyball games. Older children can log on, too, along with anyone you give access (grandparents, lawyers, babysitters). These password-protected calendars are private and available wherever you can access the Internet.

While courts in many states are now mandating this type of communication, you and your ex must both commit to its use. Start by listing your child's schedule—Kelly's math test first period or Ben's soccer practice at 3:00. Then you can add the times when you might be unavailable. And please, resist the temptation to list too much information. "Mom unavailable" is better than "Mom has a big date." Finally, on a first-come, first-served basis, the parent who marks the calendar first wins priority of the time slot.

No matter which form of communication you choose, your actions should be thoughtful, considerate, relevant, and well-timed.

11.

Divorced Homes Are Different (Sometimes)

YOUR FAMILY IS UNIQUE

As you begin to negotiate your way toward a healthy divorced lifestyle, it's important, perhaps even crucial, to let go of your expectations of what your family "should be" or, more important, "could have been." The road ahead is not the one you thought you would be on, especially alone with a child or children in tow, but it is where you are. If you accept that you can go anywhere from where you are now, then you're off on a new and exciting journey.

Divorced homes are unique, and an acceptance of that uniqueness can help you structure your "new" family (with or without another adult) so that all its members—whether there are two of you or ten—not only survive but thrive in their new family unit.

Consider yourself one of the lucky people: You have a child with you on your journey. Your child may be a lot of work right now, but as she or he grows, the physical work required to raise this child will lessen and the pleasure you receive from him or her will grow and deepen. And as your child gets older, most of your problems with your ex will diminish, giving you more time and freedom for yourself:

> When my daughter was two she developed asthma, and we were in and out of the hospital for the next few years. I decided more people should know about asthma, so I invited doctors to speak to groups of parents. The organization grew, and before I knew it I was invited to speak at hospitals. Someone at one of these events said to me, "How do you do it? You're a single mom with a full-time job and a sick child." All I could think of was, *I don't have a husband to worry about.* There was some freedom and extra time there that allowed me to grow in ways I wouldn't have if I had stayed married.

AND SOMETIMES DIVORCED HOMES AREN'T SO DIFFERENT AFTER ALL

It's understandable that you may feel overwhelmed at the thought, as well as the reality, of raising your children single-handedly. Maybe you feel devastated at the thought of not seeing your child every day. Maybe you feel overwhelmed at the responsibility of going it alone.

It would be natural for you to attribute the various problems that arise as your life unfolds to the divorce. Yet many problems that will come up for you are no different from those that come up in intact families. After all, children are still children and parents are still parents, whether they're raising children separately or together. Your divorce is not the cause of every problem, only a contributing factor to the daily challenges that parenting presents. By recognizing that some of the issues are ones you would face anyway, you can help yourself feel less overwhelmed.

> The mornings are the worst. I plop my son in front of the television with a dish of Cheerios while I take a shower with the door open so I can check on him every few seconds. After I get dressed, I try to get him dressed, which is usually a battle. He won't put on his socks. He won't wear this. He won't wear that. By the time I drop him off at pre-school and get to my office, I'm exhausted.

Sound familiar? That quote came from a happily married mother of two. Her husband gets up one hour earlier to take their older daughter to school. Even for them, parenting is difficult at times. It's exhausting for nearly everyone with young children.

> I wake my daughter up at six thirty every morning. Sometimes she doesn't get up right away, but she has her own alarm that goes off at six forty-five and she knows that if she's not up by then, I'll miss my train. After I wake her, I take a shower and she gets dressed. While I get dressed, she makes herself a sandwich that she eats in the car on

the way to school. She has to be there at eight. I drop her off and catch the eight-fifteen train. It wasn't always this way, and boy, am I glad those other days are over. I feel badly that my wife, who deals with our son each morning and drops him at pre-school, has it so much harder than I do, but that will change in time, too.

This was said by the happily married husband of the woman in the previous quote. The truth is, all parents know the physical work and scheduling challenges that having children presents. As you begin to negotiate your new life, it will be important to recognize the ways in which some things have changed because of the divorce and other things have not. This understanding will give you a more balanced view of your situation, which will allow you to be less emotional, calmer, and ultimately happier.

MONEY ISSUES GO BOTH WAYS

While divorced parents haven't cornered the market on disagreements, they certainly have their share, and as with many couples, married or otherwise, a primary conflict often revolves around money. Why? The short answer is that there usually isn't enough to go around. The long answer is more complex.

Many divorces proceed amicably as long as the monetary agreement is acceptable to both parents. When it becomes un-balanced—if one parent needs more money or the other offers less, or if your child incurs unexpected expenses, your ex can turn into a jerk in a second. And unfortunately, money problems usually do arise at some point simply because it costs between 30 percent and 60 percent more to operate two households than it does to run one. Often, too, one parent resents the other for having more money or feels taken advantage of for having to pay more.

Like all conflicts between you and your ex, when money issues arise it's critical that you keep your child out of the argument. To do this, you must first recognize if you're putting her in the middle. There are both subtle and overt ways parents do this. Consider the following:

> For her birthday my daughter wanted sneakers that cost $119, and I just couldn't afford them. She kept nagging me and dragging me into the store to see them. Finally, one day, I just burst into tears and started sobbing that if her dad gave us more money, I could buy things like that for her.

This mother, perhaps unintentionally, engaged her daughter in a money conflict with her ex. By saying that her ex was responsible for her inability to purchase the sneakers, she was essentially blaming him for not meeting their daughter's "needs." Let's see what this mother had to say after she'd thought about it a little more:

> Later, I realized it wasn't that I needed more money from her dad. I just needed more money, period. I remembered

back to when our daughter was younger, when my ex and I were still married. I didn't have $119 to spend on sneakers back then, either.

This mother came to the realization that with or without her ex, this type of problem might still occur and that dragging her ex into it was very unfair to her daughter. Had this mother said something like, "Honey, one hundred and nineteen dollars is a lot to spend on sneakers. I'm not comfortable spending that much. Is there any way you can think of to save or earn the money?" she could have avoided involving her ex.

There are also some very overt and sometimes intentional ways we engage our children in money conflicts. For example, it's really easy to answer a child's request for something with, "Ask your dad to buy it for you," or, "Doesn't your mother take care of these things?"

Tommy had his heart set on a computer for Christmas, but my cash flow was really tight. I tried to explain that it might have to wait, but he just said, "It's okay, I'll just ask Santa. Then it won't cost you anything." After hearing that, I really felt terrible. And then I saw his letter to Santa, where he wrote: "You don't have to bring me anything else, Santa. All I want is a computer and I'll be happy." I knew that I wouldn't be able to manage it this year, but I wanted so badly for him to have it. And then as I thought about it, I got angry. Why couldn't his mother buy it? Her parents had plenty of cash. I'm afraid I blew it, because when Tommy asked me if I thought Santa would bring it to him, I exploded and said, "Ask your mother! She's the one with all the money. Ask her to get it for you."

This is a terrible setup. Not only is the child left wondering what he did to provoke the anger, but by passing the buck (pun intended) this father has set it up so that in the future Tommy will be hesitant about expressing his wishes and desires to him and may look at Mom as the approachable one. In addition, Dad needs to consider whether he wants his son to get the material things he asks for whenever he asks.

It's far better to be honest with your child about money, saying that sometimes we have to wait for things that are expensive, even if we really want them, and that even Santa can't always bring children what they want exactly when they want it.

Many times the money conflicts arise because parents worry or feel guilty that they can't provide for their kids as well as their ex can. Maybe he's always taking the children to Disneyland or she has a bigger house with a pool or he just bought them iPods. This can be hard to swallow, but children are very good at differentiating between emotional support and material gain. Children know when their affections are being bought:

I grew up in a divorced home, and whenever my mom wouldn't buy me something I wanted I'd call my dad. He usually came through for me, because back in those days he had more money. I didn't think that he was nicer or better than my mom for doing it, though. I just used it as a way to get what I wanted. He used to buy me big presents for Christmas and my birthday, too, and my mom always used to accuse him of trying to buy my love. But you know what? I saw through it all. Yeah, my dad bought the dolls and bikes and cars, but my mom was there to help me with my homework.

DIFFERENT PARENTING STYLES

All parents, whether they're in an intact or divorced family, have conflicts because of different parenting styles. One parent thinks television rots children's brains; the other thinks it educates and entertains them. One parent abhors refined sugars or processed foods; the other is on a first-name basis with the dinner crew at McDonald's. One parent never leaves the child unattended; the other believes that time alone builds character and sharpens survival skills. Different styles cause disputes over scheduling, priorities, attitudes, money, discipline, food, health, safety, routines, and more.

Dissimilar approaches may not be that much of a problem in an intact home, primarily because the spouses love each other and will either agree to disagree or negotiate with each other to come up with a solution that's acceptable to both of them. In a divorce, however, when in all likelihood you've lost respect for your child's other parent, what originally might have been a mild confrontation attributed to stylistic differences can now become a major issue that adds fuel to your fire:

> My ex makes our son wear a hat whether it's cold out or not. Josh is like me and hates hats. It's getting to the point where he doesn't want to go to his mom's house because she makes him wear a hat. Most of the other kids in his class don't wear hats. He's now five years old and I think he should be able to decide for himself if his head is cold, but I just can't get through to his mother about this. It's becoming a major issue for us.

Just because your ex doesn't parent the way you do or the way you want him or her to doesn't mean he or she is wrong. Parents in strong, healthy marriages often differ on subjects like whether your son can put a hole in his earlobe or whether your daughter can wear a micromini skirt to school. Keep these stylistic differences in perspective and empower your child to deal directly with your ex as we talked about in chapter 8.

CREATING A DIFFERENT STRUCTURE

Recognizing the ways that divorced families are either the same as or different from intact families gives you the opportunity to create a different structure for your "new" family. This new structure will provide a good foundation upon which your family can grow, but building that foundation requires that you formulate different guidelines for appropriate behavior.

SEVENTEEN GUIDELINES TOWARD A SUCCESSFUL FOUNDATION

Guideline 1: *Accept Different Rules for Different Homes*

When a man and woman marry with the goal of forming a healthy family unit, individual styles of everyday living merge into a common ground. "His way" and "her way" become "their way" of doing things. When they divorce, "their way" often reverts to his way and her way. Parents may worry that this is confusing for kids, but children can rather easily accept having different rules at Mom's and Dad's house—as long as they are not asked to choose which is better:

> My daughter used to complain that her dad wouldn't let her drink soda at his house. I thought it was great that he could enforce that. So when she complained, I just empathized with her, saying things like, "Gee, it must be tough not to have soda all weekend." After a while, she stopped complaining about it. I think the fact that I accepted that her dad would have different rules made it easier for her to accept them, too.

Children will adapt to nearly any rule or routine as long as it is consistently enforced within that particular household. Eating only healthy food at one parent's house or reading for an hour before bed at the other parent's house becomes the standard for that house. While some of the rules at your ex's house may be hard for you to accept, doing so will help your child adjust far more rapidly than if you resist.

Guideline 2: Don't Make Your Child Choose Sides

Children want and need a relationship with both of their parents. When they're asked to take sides in the divorce, to choose who is better, who is right, or who is wrong, it places them in a vulnerable position. They wind up feeling disloyal and resentful. As it is, even if they're not asked to choose, many children feel that loving one parent (or a new stepparent) is being disloyal to the other one. Your children need your verbal permission to love and care for your ex, even though you no longer do.

It's also critical to acknowledge to your child the importance of her other parent. Having a parent move out can be emotionally devastating. If you create an even bigger distance between your child and her other parent by getting in the way of their relationship emotionally, it will take your child much longer to adjust to the divorce.

If the emotional distance between you and your ex is fueled by anger, your child may pick up on that and carry that anger into his or her adult relationships. Encourage both visitation and interaction between your child and his or her other parent, no matter what your feelings are.

Guideline 3: *Own Your Divorce*

One of the reasons parents intentionally or unintentionally distance their child from the other parent is because they're seeking assurance that getting divorced was the right thing to do. In making your ex the bad guy in front of your children, you may be subconsciously trying to get them to support your decision. Even if you truly believe that you were wronged, make a strong effort to dispel any kind of blame. Divorce happens. It's not a "fault" situation. It's a life situation. Don't make your children prisoners of your war. Don't ask them to contribute to your battles. They have a right to their own relationship with each of their parents.

Guideline 4: *Do Not Confide or Keep Secrets*

One of the worst things you can do to your children is ask them to keep a secret from the other parent. This puts them in an untenable position. If they keep the secret, they're being disloyal to the parent who doesn't know. If they tell, they are betraying the trust of the parent who asked them to keep the secret. It's lying in reverse.

To ask a child to withhold any reference to something he did, saw, heard, or experienced is asking him to lie. Not only will it weigh on his conscience, but it sets a precedent for lying to you as well. If you are doing something that you think your ex might object to, do not ask your child to keep it a secret, and if you think your ex will take out his anger on your child if he finds out from him, speak to your ex yourself. Don't let your child take the heat. It's not fair:

> My parents offered to take my son and me to Disney World for a much-needed vacation. But it would mean that Todd would have to miss a few days of school. I knew his dad would go nuts over the school issue and would scream at me. So I emailed him instead of calling so he would have some time to cool off before I had to face him directly, and I picked a day when he wouldn't see Todd so he wouldn't bring him into it. By the time Todd and I saw him, he had more or less accepted the trip, which gave Todd the freedom to talk openly about his excitement for meeting Mickey.

It's okay to ask your child what he or she did with Dad or Mom, but you need to ask in the same way you might if he or she had been at a friend's house or in school that day. If your true intent is to get information about your ex or if you think what your child tells you will make you angry, then don't ask.

Guideline 5: Don't Kill the Messenger or Reward the Spy

It's especially important that you not rely upon your child to carry messages to or from your ex, especially about big or sensitive issues. When you need to relay important news, call your ex directly or send an email or fax or even an old-fashioned letter. We advise against texting complicated or hot-button issues and please, if you're getting remarried, don't post it on Facebook before you tell your ex.

If your ex is using your child to deliver messages to you, politely ask him or her to stop. (And don't send that message back via your child.) If this doesn't work, empower your child to say no to your ex with a simple, "Please, Mom, if you have something to say to Dad, do it directly. Don't involve me."

> I had to tell my mom that my father was getting remarried! It's thirty years later and I'm still furious at being the messenger.

Sending messages through your child is not only unfair to your child; it opens the door for mixed messages, incorrect messages, and all sorts of triangulation and manipulation:

> For a while, I wasn't speaking to my ex, so I had our daughter make all of the pickup and drop-off arrangements. Well, one day she was on the phone with her dad and I told her to tell him that I could drop her off at four in the afternoon. There was some discussion, and then she said that I had to drop her off at six. Well, I couldn't do it that late and I didn't understand why her father couldn't take her earlier. I finally called him myself and found out that my daughter wanted to watch a show on television at four thirty, so she told him I

couldn't bring her until six. That was the last time I asked her to be the messenger!

It's also important to discourage "spying." Many times parents unintentionally reward the delivery of "confidential" information. For example, what if your child happens to tell you that his mom just broke up with her new boyfriend? Very often, parents urge their child to tell them more by saying things like, "Really? What happened?" or, not so subtly, "Tell me! Who broke up with whom and why!?"

Rewarding the delivery of this kind of information sends the wrong message to your child. You do want to validate your child's possible feelings about the situation he's relating, but you also want to be careful not to encourage him to tell you further "secrets." You might say something that focuses on him rather than on your ex and the situation. For example, if you know your child had been having fun with the new boyfriend and now seems disappointed, you can say, "I guess you're a little disappointed about that."

Finally, if you happen to be elated by your ex's misfortune or devastated by his success, leave the room for a moment until you get over it:

My son and I were building a gingerbread house one Christmas and just as we were attaching the roof he said, very innocently, "Daddy and his wife are having a baby." Well, I was so stunned that my hand slipped and knocked down one wall of the house. But I quickly pulled it together and excused myself, telling him I had to go to the bathroom. Can you imagine how hard it would have been to explain to him what was wrong if I hadn't caught myself?

Guideline 6: *Don't Give Negative Messages!*

Children gain their sense of self from identifying with each parent, so when you criticize your ex, you, in effect, criticize your child. If you say, "Your dad is stupid," your child additionally hears, "And you are stupid, too."

Most people can't suppress all of their anger all of the time, and children are very perceptive. Don't be surprised to hear your child defend his or her other parent, even if you think you're effectively hiding your feelings. Remember that your tone of voice and body language (including facial expression) communicate volumes and unless you're an excellent actor your feelings will show, at least some of the time. For this reason, it's important not to add fuel to the fire by venting about your ex in front of your child. Whereas you may think that your ex is the biggest jerk in the world, your child may feel that your ex is one of the greatest parents, or a least a good person who tries hard. Try to uphold your child's view of your ex, and vent to good friends instead.

Although criticizing your ex in front of your child is something you have control over, it may be that your ex doesn't see the need to reciprocate:

My ex-husband is constantly telling our son that women are no good, that they are not to be trusted, that they're gold diggers, and liars. I know this for a fact because he said things like this when we were married and last week he said, "You women are all alike. . . ." And, as if I needed further proof, we have a mutual friend who also hears this from him. I finally brought it up with Steven, our son, and he said that he finds those remarks very confusing. I just don't know what to do about it.

Sometimes children do come home with a message like, "Mommy says you're cheap," "Daddy says you're lazy," or, less specifically, "All women are that way," or, "Don't ever trust a man." When this happens, use it as an opportunity for an open discussion with your child. Try responding to these statements as if someone other than your ex had said them. For example, suppose your child came to you and said, "There's a kid at school who says that all women are lazy." You'd probably say to your child, "What do you think about that?" or, "Do you think that's true?" or, "How do you feel when you hear a statement like that?"

Something to keep in mind here is that while it's important to talk about your values with your child, it's not appropriate to ask your child if his other parent is saying these things. The rule of thumb is: Never ask questions you already know the answer to. So if this mother had asked Steven, "Does your dad ever make comments like . . . ?" it would likely be perceived as digging for information with an intent to criticize. It's better to keep the father out of this dialogue altogether unless Steven brought it up first. To do this, she could engage Steven in a dinner conversation about sexism, racism, and other "isms."

She could ask what he thought about comments that lump people together into categories. If Steven were to divulge that his father sometimes says things like that, Mom should acknowledge what she thinks Steven might be feeling, by saying something like, "I wonder if that feels confusing sometimes."

Know, too, that your ex may not stop thinking and speaking this way even if you ask politely, email respectfully, or hire someone to write it across the sky. The only thing you can do, and the thing you must do, is talk to your child about any feelings of being uncomfortable that he or she might have. Don't approach it as a time to set the record straight. Use it more as an opportunity for your child to express himself or herself about it. A sample conversation might go like this:

"Dad says all women are the same."

"Ah. Well, what do you think?"

"I dunno."

"Sounds like it might be a little confusing."

"Yeah. 'Cause you're not like Aunt Martha. So how can you all be the same?"

"You're definitely right about Aunt Martha and me being different! So I guess we aren't all the same."

"I hate Daddy for saying that."

"Well, could you think of a way that you could talk to him about it?"

"Yeah, right, like I'm really going to say something."

"Sounds like you feel a little nervous about that. You have good opinions, though, and you're good at being clear about them."

"I guess."

"What else might you do?"

"Well, maybe I could just put my iPod on and ignore him?"

"What do you think would happen if you did that?"

"He'd get mad and yell at me."

"So I wonder what would happen if you said something like, 'Please, Dad, can we discuss women at another time,' and left it at that?"

"Maybe. Or maybe I can just change the subject."

"Maybe! I bet you'll think of something that will help you feel more comfortable when he says those things. And you can always come to me if you're confused and we can talk about it, too."

It's also important to recognize that even though your ex may have said something nasty or off-base and even if your child has relayed the conversation to you "exactly," something could also have been lost (or gained) in the translation. Children often miss a subtle tone of voice, an obvious exaggeration, irony, sarcasm, or attempt at humor. Keep this in mind to help you keep your own feelings in check.

Guideline 7: *Beware of Cascading Consequences*

Kids will misbehave, and you will want and need to give them consequences for their actions when they do. But it's better to confine the conequences to your house rather than asking your ex to enforce them. For example, if you ask Alicia to clean her room before her dad comes over and she doesn't, don't ask him to take away her TV shows that night. It's not fair to him or to their relationship. Figure out a consequence of her action and discuss it when she returns.

On the other hand, if you found out that Tim was drinking in the woods behind your house, you may want to tell your ex about that and try to agree on a consequence that can be carried out immediately, especially now that Tim's visiting his other parent for the weekend. But you will need to agree with your ex on both the seriousness of the crime and the specific consequence in order to be successful.

Guideline 8: *Don't Parentify Your Child*

In a healthy family, the primary emotional bond is formed and maintained between the parents. Spouses in a healthy marriage do not allow children, grandparents, friends, or anyone else to come between them. Nor do they consistently take sides with these others to form a stronger coalition than the one that exists between themselves. While they might disagree at times, they know that they must consistently back each other up and meet each other's emotional needs first in order to be able to take care of the other family members.

In many unhealthy marriages (and divorces), the marital (or parenting) bond may be usurped by the children. A primary two-person relationship between a parent and a child can turn into a dangerous situation. If this bond develops in such a way that the parent begins to disclose to the child the feelings he or she would normally share with a spouse, it puts the child in the unhealthy and unfair position of "peer" with the parent. "You're Daddy's only girl now" and "Now that Daddy's gone, you're the man in the family" are classic cases of an unhealthy parent-child bond.

Relying upon your child as you would on a peer is called parentifying and it takes its toll on parents as well as children. For parents, it delays them from getting on with their social lives. Why does Mom need a boyfriend when she has the kids to hang out with? Or how can Dad afford to date when he's got to entertain the kids every weekend?

For children, parentifying gives them an unhealthy amount of responsibility for the parent's emotional well-being and can lead to more problems later on. Children may set out to "cheer Mom up" or to "calm Dad down" when it is not their job to do that.

For many reasons, you may take your time getting back into a dating scene after your divorce. That's up to you, but don't stay away because it's easier (and safer) just to hang out with the kids. Sure, your son might like to go to that movie with you, but instead of just the two of you going, have him call a friend and you call one for yourself to make it a foursome.

One guy broke up with me because he said he felt like he was dating a couple. And maybe he was right. I had my son full-time back then, and everything I did was centered on him. He was the only intimate emotional relationship I was having. My son always came first.

Parentifying and dating your children have both short- and long-term consequences. In the short term, parentified children may have an exaggerated sense of their own importance, feeling as though they are necessary for Mom or Dad's very survival. In the long term, children who assume too much responsibility for the parent may grow up to resent it and feel deprived of a carefree childhood.

These children can also grow up to be codependent, overly responsible for others, caretakers, rescuers, or incapable of allowing their own needs to be met. They may have trouble with intimacy because they are afraid that if they get close to someone, they will become responsible for that person. They may have trouble leaving their parents when they become young adults. In fact, they may never break away from the parent or the need for parental approval.

All families must have clear parent-child boundaries where a parent knows that worrying about where the money is coming from is parent business and worrying about how Santa is going to get down the chimney is kid business. When a child is used as a sounding board for financial fears or as a confidant for other adult issues, it's overwhelming. By the same token, when a parent spends too much time on the child's level, the child can lack direction and support.

Single parents may need to have children take on more responsibilities around the home, but this is not the same thing as parentifying. Children in single-parent families often develop a friendship with the parent, and that isn't bad as long as the parent's *primary need for companionship is met by another adult.* As long as clear boundaries exist between the role of the parent and that of the child, with the parent being the leader by providing routines, making decisions, and enforcing and setting limits, the child will be fine.

Guideline 9: *Don't Encourage Regression*

Some parents unintentionally encourage a child's regression or acting out after the divorce so that, in effect, they can blame the other spouse for this errant behavior. This can be a conscious or a subconscious act. If Tommy, for instance, starts sucking his thumb after the divorce, it could reinforce one parent's view that the divorce was a bad thing.

> My daughter started having nightmares after the divorce. It made me crazy. I felt so alone on the nights when we were up all night battling her imaginary monsters. But in a way, it also kind of made me feel more important. Here I was, this divorced dad with a kid who really needed me. Secretly, I sometimes enjoyed dragging into work in the morning with bags under my eyes. It made me feel like I was overcoming these huge burdens.

If you see your child regressing, get professional help for both of you. If you can get your ex to see a professional along with you, that's great, but again, don't ever count on something like that or even waste time saying, "If only he or she would get help . . ." Instead, get help for yourself and for your child.

Guideline 10: *Keep Transition Times Low-Key*

The times when your children change homes can be awkward or difficult. Making this transition is a painful reminder of the reality of the divorce: Mommy or Daddy doesn't live here anymore. To ease the transition for your child, build in as many routines as possible. The child should be told what time his other parent is coming to pick him up and what exactly will happen when the parent arrives:

> When Mom comes to get you, she'll ring the doorbell and you can answer the door. We'll put your things right there, ready to go so you don't have to hunt for anything. I'll kiss you good-bye and stand at the door to wave good-bye.

Likewise, once a child is in her new surroundings, she may need a period of time to adjust, just as you might when you arrive at work or return home after a busy day:

> I used to have a terrible time when my child returned home on Sunday nights after spending a weekend with her dad. Crying, tantrums, you name it. Then I realized that as soon as she came home, I'd dive right into a project with her. My agenda would be playing a board game or making cupcakes or something really busy. But what she really needed was just some downtime to adjust to the different dynamics, rules, and routine in our home. So now she takes a bath or we read a book or watch TV and

just hang out for a while. The tantrums have really lessened because of it.

Keeping transition times low-key also means not using them to talk to your ex about late child support checks or the personal hygiene of your ex's new boy- or girlfriend. If your ex tries to bring something up, use the "out" we talked about in chapter 4 and schedule a time when you'll call to discuss it. The focus during transition should be on your child, not on you and your ex.

Immediately following a transition, you may find that your child has some strong feelings that need to be vented. Allow your child to have those feelings, and maybe even brainstorm ways that can make the transition easier:

> My son cried so much on Sunday nights about missing his dad that we finally agreed to have him spend Sunday nights there. His dad now takes him to school on Monday mornings and I pick him up from there. It's worked well for us because they have more time together and I don't have a tired, cranky kid on Sunday night. I also get another night to make "grown-up" plans, and as a bonus, I see my ex less often!

Guideline 11: *Make a Home for Your Child*

Imagine having two homes, with some of your things in one place and some of your things in another. Surely you've traveled somewhere and wanted something that you didn't pack. It's not easy for a kid who shuttles back and forth, so it's very important for both parents to make room for the child by giving him his own space so that he doesn't feel like an intruder. Even if one parent is set up in a small apartment, it's important to give the child a drawer, a shelf, or a corner as "his." Encourage him to store his things in the space and do what he wants to personalize it. Buy special sheets for his bed that reflect his taste. Perhaps you and your child can decorate the space together, which might involve cutting out images that the child likes from magazines and taping them to a wall. The important thing is that your child feels a sense of "belonging." This is even more important if you're remarried and have other children:

My daughter started complaining that she had to sleep in the hallway at her dad's house, instead of in the bedroom with her half brother. When I asked her dad about it, he admitted that his baby had moved out of the crib and now slept in that room. Since our daughter slept there only two nights a month, they had bought a rollaway bed for her. I asked him if he had discussed this with her, and of course he hadn't. I talked to my daughter about this arrangement and she said she wouldn't mind sleeping in the hallway if it weren't a hallway. We talked about ways she and her dad could somehow fix it up to be her "room." We also talked about how she could talk to her dad. She decided that she would do it in person. We practiced an "I" statement and positive assertion that went something like, "Daddy, I feel lonely in the hallway and like I'm not a part of your family. I'd like to fix up the hall to be my room." And bless her little heart, she got through to him. I was ready to jump in and say that she would stop spending the night if he didn't resolve this, but I saved myself a lot of trouble by letting her handle it. He eventually put up a door to the hallway and she helped him paint it a color that she liked—pink, of course.

Guideline 12: *Form a Council for Cooperation*

A very successful parenting tool entails planned meetings where every family member is present. These "council" meetings are a place where everyone has an equal opportunity to express opinions and feelings or bring up problems that haven't been resolved satisfactorily.

The council is, first and foremost, a time you set aside to discuss important issues. It's helpful to set it for the same time each week and, preferably, in the same place. In addition, observing certain formalities like taking notes at each meeting and following an agenda gives the meetings some form and helps those involved know what to expect. One person (and you and your child can take turns) should lead the meeting. Leading a meeting provides a child with an important learning experience that she can use in the future.

Having an agenda for each meeting ensures that all issues are heard. During the week, as issues are raised, they can be written on a piece of paper, which will be brought to the next meeting. This gives both you and your child some time to collect your thoughts about a particular subject before you enter the discussion phase. Bedtimes, chores, cell phones, allowances, television viewing, and computer and Internet usage are all appropriate subjects. You can also use this time to listen to your child's feelings about the divorce and to figure out ways to make transition times easier on your child.

When you're trying to reach a decision at a council meeting, it's important that you don't allow the majority to rule— you might be outvoted or the result might be a stalemate. It's better to arrive at decisions by way of consensus. Reaching a consensus essentially involves brainstorming, coming up with all the possible solutions to a situation, and then sorting through them until everyone can agree on one. A consensus is sometimes viewed by parents as a difficult process because of the amount of time it takes, especially if the issue is emotional and if there are two very opposing views. But it's worth it. A consensus will save you time in the future, because when two people agree on a specific solution they're more likely to carry through with it and there will be fewer fights down the line.

One woman said during a workshop we held that she didn't see how she could have council meetings when there was only her son and herself. It's important to remember that even if you are a single parent with one child, you are a family. Having a family council meeting will send this important message to your child. The council meetings have many benefits, not the least of which is that they build a sense of cooperation because you and your child are working together on various issues as opposed to individually.

Guideline 13: *Develop New Rituals*

Holidays present problems for most divorced parents, especially during the first year, and they will probably always cause some sort of inconvenience, just as juggling two sets of in-laws can for married couples. Religious holidays are often the most difficult, and while Mother's Day and Father's Day are fairly simple, even they can cause problems if you see your child every other weekend and "your" holiday falls on the other weekend.

It helps if you can let go of that day as being the only time you can celebrate something. If you buy a turkey on the day after Thanksgiving, it's often half price and you have the whole weekend to make your special Thanksgiving dishes for a Sunday feast. A birthday can be extended to another day or weekend. Mother's Day can last a week. If you reassign your holidays, you are free to create a new ritual, which kids love, in any way you want to celebrate:

> I was so upset when my ex wanted my son on Christmas Day, because that's when Santa always came in our family. Upon reflection, however, I discovered that I really didn't like Christmas Day very much. I liked Christmas Eve and Christmas morning, but the day and night parts weren't as important to me. What I really wanted to do was get away from all the family and presents and food and just be alone. So I finally told my ex, fine, pick him up at ten, after he opens Santa's presents. I relaxed for a while and then went

to a movie. It turned into a great day, and my son had a great day, too!

Children need to belong to families and groups. They like to have a sense of structure and history. Think of these times not as ones when you can't do what you used to do but as opportunities to create new rituals that replace the old ones.

Guideline 14: *Use Trial Periods*

If you are hesitant to create a new visitation or holiday schedule with your ex, try it first. There's no law that says a change has to be permanent. But do realize that it's often harder to pull in the reins than to let them out.

When you set a precedent, set a trial period along with it: "Let's try this for the next three weeks and then evaluate." Mark it on your calendar, and even if everything is working out fine in three weeks, call your ex as you planned. (If you are in the midst of a big negotiation over visitation or money, check with your lawyer first, because you don't want to do something that may come back to haunt you.)

Guideline 15: *Remember that an Ounce of Prevention . . .*

If you and your ex are at extreme odds, prevent as many meetings, confrontations, and problems as possible. Instead of picking your child up from your ex's house, try to agree that whoever has the child must drop him off at the other's house. It's less territorial and it tells the child that you approve of the visit and that he's not being taken away but given over. Another possibility is a neutral exchange place, like school, the library, or a restaurant between both houses.

If you and your ex can't stand to be together, even for school and sporting events, arrange to sit on opposite sides of the place. One mother and father agreed that she would get the left side and he would get the right, just like guests at a wedding, when it came to school auditoriums, ballet recitals, and Little League games. Other parents split up the recitals (one goes to the dress rehearsal, the other to the performance) or alternate sporting events.

If you can arrange it, don't share clothes, toys, and other possessions. Give your child his or her own set of things, including pajamas and toothbrush, at your house (or pack a permanent set for the other parent's house, if necessary) so there is less to carry back and forth and fewer things for you to account for and argue over.

Guideline 16: *A Little Planning Can Go a Long Way*

At some point, it's likely you will begin to date again. Introducing the person you're dating to the children can be anxiety producing: Will they like her? Will he like the children? What if they can't stand each other? While there are no set rules as to how or when to introduce a new partner or "friend" to your child, a little planning can go a long way. Think through some of the basics: Given your child's temperament, would he be better off meeting someone new on his home turf or in a neutral place like a restaurant? Is your child activity oriented? If so, maybe it's best to plan an activity like going to the zoo to coincide with a first meeting. Does your child like board or computer games? Tip off your new partner by telling him or her what your child's favorites are so they begin with some common ground. Keep in mind, too, that while younger children are often more accepting of new partners than teenagers, even adult children can have issues with Mom's or Dad's new partner or spouse, so regardless of your child's age, plan ahead.

Many good books have been written about stepfamilies and how to create harmonious ones, so keep reading. You might also want to watch one of the many movies about divorce or stepparents with your child in order to start a discussion and give you an opportunity to ask and answer questions. And of course the communication techniques in this book will help as well.

Guideline 17: *Leave Well Enough Alone*

When your child is visiting her other parent, don't call, text, or email. It disrupts their time together and can suddenly change the tenor of their day, simply by interjecting yourself into their "space," even with a well-meaning, hope-you're-having-fun message. Tell your child to call you if he has a need to connect while he is away and encourage him to keep trying if you're not home instead of leaving a message:

My daughter was with her dad, so I went to the movies. When I got out and turned on my cell phone, there was a message from her left at seven fifty-two and she was crying because she missed me. By now it was ten thirty and I debated calling her back and waking her up, but I figured if the situation had gotten worse, she would have called again or her dad would have called. So I waited until the morning to return her call. That was very hard for me, but I knew it was the right thing to do and that calling her back might start her missing me all over again.

YOUR CHILD'S NEEDS AND RIGHTS

It's easy to get caught up in the hassles of the divorce and the battles of custody and forget that your child has needs. She needs to be loved by you for who she is, not for what she does or how she behaves, and she needs a relationship with both parents. Because of this relationship, your child needs to be protected from your arguments with your ex. And inclusive of that relationship, your child needs to feel part of both families—yours and your ex's. This means creating an environment where she feels wanted and welcomed, whether you're the custodial or non-custodial parent.

Your child also has rights. He has the right to experience all of his feelings and thoughts, both positive and negative. And he has the right to express those feelings and thoughts to you, even if you don't agree with them. Your child has the right to ask questions and receive honest answers from you. Your child has the right to be treated respectfully in all circumstances. This means talking to him in the respectful way that you would talk to another adult, even when you're angry with him. And finally, your child has the right to and the need for a childhood unburdened by your responsibilities. Walt Disney once said that to a child every day is like an enormous gift, just waiting to be unwrapped. As parents, we are human and we make mistakes. But don't make the mistake of squashing that gift.

12.

Living (and Dating) on the Bright Side

HEALING AFTER DIVORCE

Take Care of Yourself

The bottom line is this: Divorce sucks. Accepting this fact allows you to process what you're going through, to heal, and, finally, to move on. You will undoubtedly meet divorced people who never seem to get over the hurt, anger, and devastation of the breakup. The difference between people who live happily ever after and those who don't lies in whether they've taken the time to heal, to examine their lives and learn from whatever they've been through, and then to make educated choices and move through to the brighter side of life.

Healing takes time. It also requires that you be willing to take care of yourself, and it can be difficult to give yourself permission to do this, especially after the trauma of a divorce. Because of added financial pressure, less time with the children, and more time spent juggling schedules, you may feel either frustrated that there simply is not time left over for you or guilty for taking the time you need to recover:

> I know I need to take care of myself better. Sometimes I even forget to eat. It's just that I feel like I'm constantly picking up the pieces of disasters, and between working and caring for the kids I'm so busy that I don't have time even to stop to think, much less take time out for me. And yet I know if I did, I'd probably feel better and get more done.

Now, more than ever before, it's important to make time for you. Think about the words that some 2 million Americans hear every day—words that could save their lives and the lives of their children. During the takeoff of every commercial airplane flight in America, the pilot says, "If the cabin loses pressure, an oxygen mask will drop down in front of you. Place the mask over your mouth and tighten the straps before you attempt to help your child or anyone else."

Think about it for a minute. This procedure makes sense. In a crisis, we function better if we take care of our own immediate needs first. Then we are more equipped to help others. During your divorce especially but also throughout your life as a parent, this means eating enough food, getting enough sleep, and doing whatever it takes to help you become stronger. This may mean hiring a babysitter to take care of the kids one night a week, phoning or having coffee with a sympathetic friend, or going for a long drive by yourself. It certainly means assessing the things that give you, as an individual, joy and then integrating them into your daily or weekly plans.

Create Balance

As you begin to accept your divorce and start to heal and grow from it and then determine what specific activities help you feel good about yourself, remember that balance is important. Just like a balanced diet helps you maintain a healthy body, a balanced lifestyle brings a sense of order and proportion to one's life, giving you the freedom to attain new goals and experience peace of mind and body.

Balance your new "jerk-free" lifestyle with equal parts of work and play, with giving and receiving, time with friends or family and time alone. Beware of excess as well as neglect. If surfing the Web helps you relax, for example, remember that there's a difference between using a relaxation tool and abusing one. Make sure that computer time is balanced with people time.

When you feel yourself going down the path of extremes, stop for a moment and look around. Then turn around. Call a friend or family member or your therapist for help without feeling guilty about asking. People love to help people and there is no shame in needing a hand to help or an ear to listen once in a while.

Allow Yourself to Grieve

Grief is a normal reaction to divorce. Whether you sought the divorce or your ex did, it's likely that you will go through the grief process first described by Elisabeth Kübler-Ross. The stages include denial ("This is not happening to me"), anger ("How dare he/she? What a jerk!"), bargaining ("Maybe if I agree to ___, he/she will come back"), depression ("Oh my God, this is really happening. I can't do this"), and acceptance ("It's time to move on. That part of my life is over").

The stages of grief are not linear. One day you may find yourself lying around, wondering why you don't have the energy to find the remote control to change the channel on the television. The next day you may find a sock of your ex's and angrily burn it in the kitchen sink. The following day you may clean your house, throw out all of his or her old things, and think, *Well, gee, things aren't so bad after all.* And then you may go back to a former stage or experience a stage you haven't thus far.

Someone once compared the stages of grief to an elevator: It stops on the first floor, goes up to the fifth, back to the second, up to the fourth, and so on. Because of grief's unpredictability, it can be a frustrating process, often infused with guilt ("I must have done something wrong") and shame ("I'm so embarrassed that I didn't see what a jerk he/she was earlier").

None of these feelings (with the exception of acceptance) are easy, nor are they ones we would ever choose to have. That being said, allowing yourself to feel these feelings without suppressing or denying them is an essential part of moving forward. Think about it this way: When a baby learns to walk, she would probably rather skip the parts where she falls down, skins her knee, bumps her head, and so on. But these are a part of learning, growing, and moving through an important developmental stage.

When you experience one of the "bumps and bruises" in the aftermath of your divorce, take a deep breath. Remember that grief won't last forever. Allow yourself to cry: It's been said that tears are to the soul what soap is to the body. And know that it's only an emergency if you can't breathe.

Acknowledging your grief and loss will not only help you move past these feelings, but it will also keep them from lingering deep within only to resurface and sabotage your new relationships or your continuing relationship with your ex:

> I couldn't believe this single mom I dated occasionally. I had rented a country house and it was the weekend before the season started and I had the house all to myself. I didn't have my son that weekend and she didn't have hers, so I called her and invited her to spend the weekend, and she said yes. But then on Friday morning she called and told me that she had just received a letter from her ex's lawyer and was really upset. She canceled, saying she really wanted to spend the weekend drafting a response to his letter. I couldn't believe it. She chose to blow off a weekend in the country for a letter to her ex. That was the last time I ever asked her out. I heard recently that three years later, she's still not divorced.

Unstick Yourself

Sometimes you might feel as though you're stuck in a particular stage of the grief process. When this happens, some people have found it helpful to have a list of things to do that bring immediate rewards. Put small jobs on the list—jobs that carry with them a sense of accomplishment, like polishing silver or doing a load of laundry. If you don't have the energy to clean your entire home, it's enough to just do the dishes or empty the garbage during this distressing time. You may not have the energy to run five miles, but a walk around the block can clear the fog from your brain. And maybe you don't have time for that round of golf, but how about hitting a bucket of balls at the local driving range? Or buying that magazine that suddenly appeals to you and finding a quiet bench or coffee bar where you can read it? Then cross this activity off the list and pat yourself on the back for being able to do one positive thing for yourself:

After we split up, I moved into my own apartment, and it was so depressing at first. I could afford only a one-bedroom apartment and I wanted to have a bed for Ben when he came on weekends, so I ended up getting two twin beds. I hadn't slept in a twin since college. Anyway, I was always depressed whenever I walked into the bedroom. Plus it was a mess, with clothes all over the place. I felt really stuck, like things would be this way forever. Then a friend suggested that I buy a king-sized bedspread and push the beds together when Ben wasn't there. She went with me to buy sheets and curtains and blankets in all these great-looking colors. After that, I started making the bed each day and every week I'd switch to a different color of sheets. I couldn't believe the difference this made. Now, when I'm feeling sad about being single, I change the sheets to give the room a different look. It helps a lot.

Start to Forgive

Your ex may have done things or said things to you during and after your marriage that you feel very unforgiving about. You can't change history, but you can change your attitude about it. Forgiveness doesn't mean that you approve of what your ex did or didn't do. It means that you no longer want to dwell on it or remember it every time you speak to or see your ex. Think of the energy that recalling the past takes out of you. When you forgive, you have the option of putting that energy to use in a more positive way.

Forgiving your ex is not the same as letting him or her off the hook. It's akin to cutting the line. It's an act that frees you. When you forgive your ex, you let go of the past instead of being dragged along by it. Releasing your anger lightens your heart and loosens your emotional ties to your ex. It also makes it more likely that you will eventually be able to develop a more harmonious relationship with him or her.

Initially, it may feel as though your current relationship with your ex will last forever, that you'll never be able to forgive him or her. But remember what we've said several times already: The words "always" and "never" are inaccurate and immobilizing. So is the word "forever."

Embrace Change

The one constant in life is change, so while things may be hard right now, nothing lasts forever. The current arguments that you have with your ex may feel as though they're all-encompassing and critically important, but they will abate over time. In addition, as your child matures she will have her own opinion about things and, especially if you've empowered her to talk to you and her other parent, she'll assert herself in the decision making, which will also be a force for change:

> We separated right after my daughter was born. My ex and I talked, argued, negotiated on every bit of parenting—when to feed her, which playgroup she should go to, where she should go to school, homework, you name it. But as she got older, we talked less, just because the seeds we had planted, so to speak, had grown into a beautiful garden. When our daughter had an issue with either of us, she spoke up. And now she's a gorgeous young woman who will graduate from college soon. I'm still not particularly fond of my ex, but our contact is minimal compared to what it used to be.

Forgiving your ex and eventually developing a compatible, or at least neutral, relationship with him or her may take a long time. But as you rack up months and years in your new post-marital lifestyle, your children will get older, your parenting skills will develop, and you'll get on with your life. Your child's other parent will probably be there twenty, thirty, and even forty years down the road, so don't ever give up on the goal of creating a harmonious relationship with him or her. And remember, any time and energy you spend hating and being angry at your ex will ultimately take a toll on you without effecting any positive changes in your ex or your relationship.

Be Positive

Both Eastern and Western religious traditions have long professed that we have partial but substantial responsibility for the things that happen to us. This idea was popularized by Dale Carnegie in the 1930s and '40s and has continued to inspire and change lives in the work of motivational speakers like Tony Robbins, Stephen Covey, and, we're willing to bet, the latest and most popular self-help guru today.

Partial but substantial responsibility means that the way we look at life influences what happens to us in our lives. While some people take this to an extreme, claiming that we have full responsibility for what happens (for example, if we get cancer we must have "attracted" that cancer to us in some way), we certainly wouldn't go that far. We do believe, however, that we have a choice about how to look at life. We can see the glass as half-full instead of half-empty. It simply requires a shift in perspective.

When we choose to see life's glass as half-empty and look at life in a negative way, we're more likely to speak negatively and to act in negative ways. This influences the world around us. People are less likely to want to spend time with us and we're more likely to make negative choices, believing that nothing we do will matter. In short, when we think negatively our lives become more negative. On the other hand, a shift from negative to positive thought causes us to make better choices because we believe that we have the power to control at least some of what happens in our lives. In turn, people enjoy being around us because we have a cheerful, outgoing, and positive demeanor.

It's not always easy to see negative situations in a positive light. Like most things, it takes practice to turn negative thoughts and phrases like "It will never work" into positive ones like "Let's give it a try." Yet when we turn "It's a waste of time" into "Think of the possibilities" and "I don't know what to do" into "I have so many choices," it will create positive opportunities in our lives. With practice, soon you'll be hearing yourself say, "Yeah, my ex used to make me crazy and he still acts like a jerk sometimes. But I've got better things to do than waste my time and energy on him." Similar to lifting weights and building your strength, when you start small and practice daily you move from small positive thoughts to a more positive lifestyle:

> I've always said that the upside of divorce is every other weekend off. When my kids are with their dad for the weekend, I can do anything I want. Plus, for me, living well is the best revenge.

Encourage Each Other

Similar to thinking positively, a significant and healthy part of the healing process involves encouragement. To encourage means to instill with courage or to build confidence. Both you and your child or children need strength during this time, so take the time to encourage your child or children and yourself by noticing and mentioning the positive things that each of you did on a daily basis. Tell yourself, "I'm proud that I did ___ today," and "I recognize that I accomplished ___."

A few kind words may be just what you need to get you through the difficult times. Be your own best friend and acknowledge to yourself those things you've done right.

In the same respect, encourage your child by saying, "I noticed that you ___ this week," "I saw that you did ___ well," "I bet you're proud of yourself that you ___." Encouraging words help people feel closer to each other, and you'll be surprised to see that your child will pick up on your encouragement and give you a few encouraging words of her own.

Don't Look Back

Sometimes, dealing with the complexities of life after divorce can make you feel as though you'll never get past it. There may be days when your ex exasperates you so much that it feels all-consuming. You feel like things will never change and thoughts of revenge fill your mind and cloud your thinking. Other times, you might dwell in regret, wishing you could turn the clock back. Maybe you feel that if you'd only done something differently, the marriage wouldn't be over.

While it's true that sometimes people do get back together, try to remember that if your ex was unable to meet your needs during your marriage, it's unlikely that he or she will be able to meet them now. Some say it's like putting spoiled milk back in the fridge. The milk will still be bad when you take it out.

Similarly, some people don't necessarily want to get back together with their ex, but they hold on to the fantasy that now that they're divorced their ex will change. This, too, can keep you from moving forward:

> Everything was fine until my ex remarried, had a few kids, and didn't have enough money to go around. He turned into a real jerk about child support and we wound up in court. He wanted to know what my boyfriend contributed to our living expenses so that he could claim I needed less support. Every time he brought this up, I saw red. We had struck a bargain ten years before on a set amount. I wasn't asking for more.
>
> Well, after a particularly grueling day in court, my boyfriend took my child and me to a movie that I really wanted to see, but I couldn't pay attention to the movie. I just kept beating myself up over what had gone on in court. Why didn't I say this, I wish I hadn't said that, how could he say such a thing, he's a jerk and a liar. Then it hit me: Regardless of how often I replayed this in my head, he's going to do what he's going to do, and the longer I thought about it, the longer he had the power. Then I realized I had a choice—I could stew or I could forget about him and enjoy the movie. Once I consciously decided to let it go, I felt like I had the upper hand. I was able to relax and enjoy the movie.

It's important to manage your expectations. While your ex may change and while some people do get back together, it's probably better to assume this won't happen. We're not asking you to think negatively, just realistically. Your primary goal should be to have a great life. You can still have a good day, enjoy your child, and ultimately find happiness, whether your ex is acting like a jerk or a responsible person. Your happiness is not dependent upon someone else.

Keep Your Sense of Humor

Abraham Lincoln once said, "Most people are as happy as they make up their minds to be." Like happiness, a sense of humor is something you can choose and develop. And there is humor in almost every situation if you look hard enough. When you find the humor in life, you will feel lighter and brighter.

Steven M. Sultanoff, Ph.D., the past president of the Association for Applied and Therapeutic Humor, recommends five things that will keep humor in your life and help you "learn how to live a longer, healthier life through laughter." He says on his site www.humormatters.com:

1. *Seek humor daily: Read a joke, cartoon, comic strip, listen to a comedian, watch a sitcom, etc.*
2. *Look to the humor around you: See the world through humor eyes. For example, consider the freeway sign north of the San Diego Airport that reads,* **"Cruise Ships: Use Airport Exit."**
3. *Carry a toy or prop: For example, I carry a clown nose*

with me everywhere I go and my watch runs backwards.
You should see the smiles when I show it to others asking
for the time.

4. *Subscribe to a joke service: The Internet is filled with*
   these.

5. *Share (in person, if possible) a favorite funny daily with*
   a favorite friend: This will help keep you connected!

MOVING FORWARD

Make New Friends

Often in a divorce the friends get divvied up between the husband and the wife as if they were household goods. This can feel devastating, adding to your already substantial feelings of loss. That's why it's so important that you make an effort to reach out to new people and form new friendships.

At first, you may understandably gravitate most comfortably toward other divorced parents. This is natural because other divorcées can help you process your own divorce. And some of these people will become friends for life. Keep in mind, though, that if your friendships with other divorced people are only serving to help you rehearse and rehash bad feelings, you'll want to enlarge your circle.

As you begin to meet new people, ask yourself whether you're looking for a friend, a sexual companion, a parenting partner, or a family network. Rarely can one person serve these

LIVING (AND DATING) ON THE BRIGHT SIDE

multiple roles. Maybe you'll have one friend who is someone to talk to about business issues; maybe another can be a sexual companion and still another might be a parenting partner. Perhaps another single parent can share in some of the work of parenting with you, just as you might be able to serve in that role for him or her. As you begin to make new friends, you may find that you're moving toward a readiness to date again.

Reentering the social scene and going outside of your "comfort zone" after your divorce may feel akin to jumping into an ocean of sharks, but keep in mind that there are many ways to meet people. Some people enroll in adult education classes, take up a hobby, enter bike-a-thons, or volunteer for a cause. Others tell their friends that they'd like to meet people. Some people meet through their place of worship or neighborhood community groups. Still others join a book club or become part of the PTA at their child's school. Some advertise on the Internet.

Remember: Practice Makes Perfect

After years of marriage, you may find that you need a little practice with dating and forming new relationships. That's natural, and while some people may feel embarrassed at the need for practice, think of it as honing your skills, just as one might practice a golf swing or the piano. Your golf game or your musical abilities will not improve if you don't put time and energy into doing it right.

In addition, to attract quality friends or partners one must be a quality person. Take a look at yourself and take ownership of whatever qualities or habits may have contributed to a failed relationship. Once you recognize the part you've played, you have the ability to change—for the better.

New Partners Must Like Kids

As you begin to date, be aware that some single parents you meet may want to get overly involved too quickly and for the wrong reasons. This is another excellent reason to take things slowly. Start with coffee; move up to brunch; take in a movie. When you take your time without rushing into things, you have the opportunity to get to know whether the person you're dating is one that you're dating for the right or the wrong reasons. Likewise, you'll discover the reasons behind him or her wanting to date you.

Another thing to take into consideration as you're exploring a dating relationship with someone is whether or not your new friend has a child or children. It's likely that you'll have more in common with someone who does. As your relationship moves forward, include conversations about parenting. Different parenting styles can make it exceptionally difficult to blend families and may prove to be a "deal breaker" down the line.

If you're dating someone who doesn't have children, you'll want to talk about what his or her thoughts, dreams, and wishes are about having a child. How does he or she feel about being a stepparent? Does he or she want a biological, adoptive, or foster child of his or her own?

Obviously, these conversations are not appropriate for a first or second date. Still, keep in mind that if you meet someone who doesn't want to be a stepparent, you should move on quickly. Thinking that you'll change him or her is as futile as believing you can change your ex:

> One man I dated had a daughter who was my daughter's age, and that was terrific, but he didn't want to be a stepfather. I was incredulous—I thought I'd found someone who enjoyed kids and would enjoy stepparenting as much as he enjoyed being a parent. But it wasn't meant to be. He just couldn't wrap his head around that role. Luckily, I found out fairly soon in our dating relationship and didn't make any false assumptions. He later found a woman who was childless and who wanted to remain so, and I found a terrific man who didn't have kids of his own but who dotes on my daughter as if she's his own.

Consider New Resources

Only you can decide when it's time to date and if you're open to dating anyone, only a parent, only a divorced person, or only a never-been-married person. While it used to be difficult for people to meet someone who had the specific characteristics they were looking for, online dating has changed all that. In fact, many people have had tremendous success with online dating for the very reason that it's easy to sort by these characteristics.

There are dozens of books that give tips and advice about the dos and don'ts of these online matches, and we encourage you to read one of them. Our advice, however, is to be up-front about being a divorced parent and to give the introduction a chance before you decide whether or not it's for you:

> I met this woman online and as we were chatting, but before I could tell her I had a daughter, she started telling me that she was shopping for a dining table for two with two chairs, because that was all that would fit in her apartment. All I could think of was, *Where would Amanda sit?* I almost didn't meet her until my sister pointed out that Amanda didn't need a place to sit at her apartment and that if things were working out, we could all sit at mine. I realized that I wasn't giving it a chance, and retrospectively I think I was looking for things that would prevent me from meeting her because I was nervous.

Don't Spring a New "Friend" on Your Child

Introducing your new "friend" to your child can be complicated. Most experts and been-there-done-that parents suggest you wait until you have established a solid relationship with the new man or woman before you bring him or her home for cookies and milk. Keep the first introduction brief and informal.

Finding the time to date, the money for child care, and someone to whom you feel attracted may seem like an impossible task, but single parents succeed at this all the time. The one common quality of successful unions is that they feel like things just "click," that there's a natural and comfortable quality that doesn't feel forced or rushed. Forcing a square peg in a round hole is rarely satisfying and needing it "today" can be a recipe for disaster:

> I was often driven by a sense of urgency to date when my kids were with their dad. I'd go to a party on a Saturday night and meet a guy and get all excited about him. Then I'd start thinking, *I have both kids next weekend, and one kid the weekend after, and both the weekend after that, and if I don't sleep with this guy tonight,* I'll have to wait a month! I became overwhelmed by this urgency to have sex and often had it too soon. But then I met Scott, and the first thing he did was make a date for brunch the next day. And then he made another date and another. My urgency turned to a positive energy and we just figured it out as we went along. It reminded me that dating takes time and when it's right it just sort of works out.

As you begin to date, remember to breathe and take things one step at a time. Part of meeting Mr. or Ms. Right is that it will feel natural. You won't have to twist yourself into a knot, jump through hoops, or fend off disappointment over and over again. And remember: All parents juggle their social lives, whether they're divorced or not; it's just a part of being a parent.

Give Life a Chance

In life, especially in the middle of a crisis like a divorce, it can be easy to allow your anxiety and other negative feelings to prevent you from moving forward. A thoughtful approach, even if it's in retrospect, allows you to give life—and happiness—a chance. Plus, it's really true what they say—kids grow up fast and your best days are ahead.

Finally, in the spirit of looking at the glass half-full, try not to dwell on what you don't have. Instead, look at what you do have, because whether you number two or ten, you are a family. And being in a family, no matter what its size or shape, is a gift. Cherish it.